It Wasn'ı
After All

It Wasn't So Bad After All

J. Frost

The Pentland Press Limited
Edinburgh • Cambridge • Durham • USA

© J. Frost 1996

First published in 1996 by
The Pentland Press Ltd.
1 Hutton Close
South Church
Bishop Auckland
Durham

British Library Cataloguing in Publication Data.
A catalogue record for this book is available
from the British Library.

ISBN 1 85821 376 2

Typeset by CBS, Felixstowe, Suffolk
Printed and bound by Antony Rowe Ltd., Chippenham

Dedicated to
Marjorie
and her mother
Mrs Julie Reeves Wood

to
Dr Gordon Ames
and his wife Joan

and
to Ted my husband

ACKNOWLEDGEMENTS

I should like to thank Lena Glover, who said the story should be written, and Leslie Taylor, who patiently helped me to complete it.

FOREWORD

Inside every one of us there is a story waiting, often begging, to be told. Yet it takes extraordinary courage to confront the ghosts of one's past, to put pen to paper and tell it like it is.

Jess Frost migrated to Australia almost half a century ago, and she now considers this country to be her home.

With her passionate sense of duty and self-discipline also seen is the warm, caring nature of an intelligent woman with a sense of humour fit to kill.

Born in England in 1918, Jess's early years were spent growing up in the comfortable lifestyle provided by her paternal grandfather. To Jess, early childhood was an idyllic existence, the only real cloud being her parents' lack of demonstrative affection towards their children and each other.

By the mid 1920s, the death of Jess's grandfather coupled with the onset of the Great Depression, saw the family's fortunes suddenly plummet. Forced to sell up the big house, life became a series of heartbreaking moves from one rented lodgings to another, always smaller, always seedier. With little income and plenty of mouths to feed, arguments soon replaced the laughter.

Eventually however life began to improve, the family's saviour coming in the form of a small, semi-detached countryside cottage known as 'Rabbit Pit Cottage', where plenty of fresh air, home-grown vegetables and resident rabbits provided a simple but healthy diet. Just the same, discipline was harsh and the eternal drought on parental hugs and kisses did little to counteract the sadness which often weighed heavy in Jess's heart.

Yet, as a toddler clings to its favourite teddy, Jess also carried a very special dream that bridged all hurts, all disappointments, all the unanswered questions of her childhood – one day she would become a nurse and she would help make people better. With little formal education and the unbending social structure of the pre-war British class system, few held any hope of Jess achieving her dream.

But what no-one had anticipated was that while a tough childhood may have taken its toll, it had also helped create a stronger and more resilient young woman, one whose passion for nursing would see her absolutely determined to beat the odds. But it wouldn't happen over-night.

Initially bundled off into domestic service, Jess later found alternative employment in a factory working twelve hours a day painting heavy wooden drink crates for 1/3 a hundred. At week's end, she would hand her pay packet to her mother, and receive a small amount back as pocket money. Eventually she managed to land a position as a hospital domestic and while it was still a far cry from her chosen profession, Jess had finally got her foot in the door – nothing would stop her now.

In the years that followed, hard work, dedication and sheer determination were to pay off. Not only would this remarkable young woman complete and pass her training to become a State Registered Nurse at a prestigious London hospital, but she would also go on to become a State Certified Midwife.

All of this would take place in and around London amidst the turmoil and heartbreak of World War Two.

Even today, it isn't difficult to imagine Jess and her fellow nurses doing their rounds as District Nurses in war-torn London; walking through busy streets, conspicuous in their trademark London Hospital uniform of bonnet with large velvet bow in front and coat which billowed out at the sides.

It Wasn't So Bad After All is the story of a young woman who never gave up on her dream, who even in her darkest moments was determined to give it her very best shot. It is about personal hardships and joys, class distinction and bridging gaps, love and heartbreak and told without the distractions of flowery adjectives.

But it is also a fascinating historic account of wartime nursing in London, told with great compassion and wonderful humour. For a woman who insists she has always had difficulty expressing herself, Jess Frost has put together, beautifully, a story that will warm your heart.

Karen Matthews
Women's Editor
Geelong Advertiser
Victoria, Australia

CHAPTER 1

It is mid-morning. The sun is warm, and I am resting in my favourite armchair in the sun-room. How peaceful it is! The silence is broken now and then by the birds as they fight over a crust of bread I had thrown out earlier, and there is the sound of the traffic in the distance. My husband Ted and I are enjoying our twilight years – he recently celebrated his ninetieth birthday. He potters here and there; there's always something to do and he welcomes the challenge of helping others. We've had a busy life. I think of the past and remember so well that as a small child I was determined that I would be a nurse one day.

We lived with Grandfather in the big house. He had been a lonely old man after Grandmother died so Mother and Dad with Dorothy, my older sister, and baby John moved in to care for him. There were many rooms in the big house so it was easy to hide if I saw Grandfather coming – I was afraid of him. He was a very big man with a long grey beard, and he only sent for me when he wished me to recite. The only poem I knew was, 'The three little kittens who lost their mittens'. He never spoke, just stared at me and didn't smile, then said, 'Off you go.' That's how it was with him; he had very little to do with us children. He spent most of his time in his greenhouse – perhaps he talked to the plants there.

Grandfather had six children: three boys and three girls. As a small child I knew very little about them, but they did appear later when I grew up. Dad was his second child; he always dressed well, wore a bowler hat and carried an umbrella when he went out. Apparently he had been a bachelor gay before he met Mother – she must have caught his eye, even though she was seventeen years younger. She was an attractive woman and I believe he was very proud of her. Were they in love? I don't remember seeing them kissing, hugging or even holding hands.

Dorothy arrived early in the marriage and I followed two years later, then John arrived. No longer a gay bachelor, Dad had to curb his activities; he wouldn't have found this too easy.

Dad kept a wonderful veggie patch and his prize possessions were his cucumbers, which he grew under small glass frames. Obviously he was like his father who also loved his garden. I spent a lot of time with him and would sit on one of the frames to watch him. He had warned me that I mustn't sit on the glass but of course I did, breaking a pane and cutting my foot very badly, and getting numerous glass splinters in my knees. I was taken to the doctor in a push-chair and he put six stitches in my foot. This was very painful and nothing was given to ease it. The doctor said I was very brave, but Dad was annoyed, saying that it would not have happened, had I done as I was told. My foot was very sore and I wanted Dad to put his arm around me, but he didn't.

The daily help was a young girl about fifteen years old. She didn't care for us, but did take us for walks, which we loved. Sometimes we visited the local bakery as her boyfriend worked there.

At the back of the house were stables and there our two horses lived, Tommy and Bessie. They were our work-horses, but they were also members of the family, well fed and healthy. I loved them. I believe Dad had been involved with race-horses at some stage in his life; he certainly knew how to handle them.

Dad was a house-to-house greengrocer. He owned two carts, and sometimes Mother would join him on his round. As his produce was always fresh and his prices reasonable, he was very popular. The horses always knew when Mother was in charge because they got extra tit-bits. They knew the district well and were always reliable. When work finished, they were fed and released to the field at the back of the house. Dinner over, Dad would have a rest before doing his book work. Early morning would find him away to the market. The horses came to the back door for a lump of sugar before they were put into the cart.

One evening there was a commotion in the stables, which was most unusual as the horses always settled down well. It appeared that Tommy had bitten Bessie. Dad scratched his head and wondered why this had happened but we all knew that Tommy was jealous of Bessie, sensing that she was Dad's favourite; however, he hadn't shown aggression before. Dad separated them but a few days later Tommy again showed his aggression and while Mother was giving Bessie her lump of sugar, he

2

lashed out, kicking Mother in the stomach. She was pregnant at the time and was in dreadful pain. Dad sent for the ambulance and she was admitted to hospital.

I don't know why, but I had always imagined that hospitals were holes in the ground. How relieved I was to find that they were just large buildings above ground! Mother did lose the baby and it was some time before she fully recovered.

Despite that episode Tommy was given a reprieve – Mother was very forgiving. All went along smoothly for some time, then one morning Dad found Bessie dead in her stall. It was a shattering experience for him; indeed, we were all very upset. Mother told us to stay inside while Bessie was taken away but I watched through the window. Bessie was dragged by a chain round her neck into a cart. Tears flowed down my face – what a dreadful thing to happen! Poor Bessie, we loved her so.

Tommy disappeared after this, Dad and Mother wouldn't say where, but they used a motor-van from then on. Being a little over five years old, it did make a big impression on me and I realised that unhappy things can, and do, happen in the animal world as well.

For my birthday that year I was given a beautiful doll. I was told that it had belonged to my grandmother. It was beautiful, with long blond hair, and was dressed in the most exquisite white gown made of pure cotton, trimmed with lace. I was so very proud of her, and I took her everywhere in my push-cart, but one day I left her at the bottom of the garden where Dorothy, John and I were throwing stones just to see how far we could throw them. One hit my doll in the face, smashing it. I don't know which stone it was but I was responsible. So many tears! I was reprimanded, of course, and the doll was taken away. I never saw it again, nor was I ever given another one. The tears flowed freely for days.

CHAPTER 2

One glorious day when I was about eight years old Mother said we could visit and play with friends, and after an early lunch my sister, young brother, and I set out. The countryside was lovely, we enjoyed walking and did a lot of it. Our friends lived in a delightful old cottage with a thatched roof. They had three children who were round about the same age as us and they went to the same school. Our families had been friendly for a number of years.

We had a lovely time and the home-made cakes were delicious. What a treat for us to enjoy someone else's cooking! Of course, Mother was a good cook too but Mrs Eagles' cakes always seemed better somehow. Soon it was time to return home; Mother had told us not to be late and we knew to disobey was to expect a punishment. My sister Dorothy decided there was plenty of time and she stayed there; fearing the wrath of Mother, we left her. We were carefree and happy, our tummies full. John raced on ahead into the long grass, which was plentiful on the side of the road, but suddenly, he stopped, yelling that he was stuck. I rushed towards him but I got stuck also. We were terrified and screamed as loudly as we could; John had a look of horror on his face as he was sinking fast. Nearby there were a few scattered cottages and a man from one of these, hearing the noise, came running towards us. He yelled for us to stay as still as possible, and went to get help. He hurried back with another man, carrying a long ladder between them which they placed across the bog. Cautiously one of the men crawled along, reaching John first. He pulled him out but it wasn't easy, as he was stuck well above his waist; the thick black smelly sludge oozed from his clothes. Then it was my turn; as I watched, I sobbed. 'What will Mother say?'

We were taken to the man's cottage and there we were bathed in a big tin bath in front of the fire. I hadn't seen one of these tin baths before, at the big house we had a bathroom. We were dressed in an assortment of

4

clothes. I didn't like the socks I was wearing as they had holes. After a hot drink we were taken home. Mother was shocked when she heard what had happened; she knew full well that those bogs were very dangerous. It was said that many animals had disappeared after falling in. I learnt a lesson that day. When he heard about it, Dad said that those bogs should be fenced.

As the weeks passed I became aware of a very tense atmosphere in the home. Grandad had fallen and had broken his arm, but I wasn't aware that his general health had deteriorated somewhat, and a few weeks later he died. In a way I missed him; he had been part of my life in those early formative years. I had learnt many poems so that I would be able to recite to him, should he wish it. His death brought so many changes – somehow, that house was my Camelot: a golden time, a good time.

Conditions changed rapidly, it appeared that there were many family arguments which caused much unhappiness. I didn't understand it at all, but I heard that the house was to be sold. Our home was to be sold – how could Mother and Dad let this happen? It was unbelievable but very soon we were packing. Mother and Dad looked most unhappy. The domestic was given the sack; I think she was sad that she was leaving. She had been with us quite a long time and she gave us a big hug.

There were strangers milling around and most of the lovely furniture was taken away. I watched sadly as our house was being emptied; all the things I had loved were being taken away.

Mother and Dad must have been devastated seeing some of their loved pieces disappear.

We didn't leave the town but moved into a small terraced house, one of seven joined together. Ours had only five rooms, two rooms downstairs and three bedrooms upstairs. There wasn't a bathroom – how would we bath? Surely, not in one of those big tin baths! We were cramped and unhappy. Mother was crosser than usual, and Dad tried so hard to continue his vegetable round. Unfortunately, there was nowhere to park the van, so it had to stay in the street, and there wasn't the clientele in that area. He was very despondent.

We children attended the local school. I was nine years old and I loved school; we made many friends.

There was no privacy and the neighbours on either side were noisy and aggressive, and they were always asking to borrow things. One girl about my age asked Mother to give them a drop of oil for their lamp. 'We ain't got none,' she said, 'and we ain't got no candles either.' She was very dirty and had a runny nose, which she kept wiping on the back of her hand.

'Haven't you got a handkerchief?' I asked her but, by the way she looked at me. I don't think she knew what it was. What a traumatic change it was and what a lasting effect it made on a child's mind!

The young fellow next door had a very old motorbike, and he was always tinkering with it. It was very noisy and leaked a lot of petrol. One afternoon there was quite a commotion outside and, looking through the window, I saw that his hand was covered with blood. He was yelling at the top of his voice, 'I've cut off the top of my finger.' He had caught it in the chain of the motorbike. There was blood everywhere; Mother always said a little blood can make a lot of mess. Nevertheless, she bandaged the stump and someone took him to hospital. I picked up the piece of finger, which fascinated me – it was very squashy. I gave it to Mother, who just smiled; she had heard me say so many times that I would be a nurse when I grew up. Today the stump would have been rejoined with micro-surgery. How things have changed!

CHAPTER 3

One day I was told that we were going to have another baby. This was exciting news as I loved babies. I remember answering the door one evening, and I smiled at the nurse who stood there holding a large bag.

'Have you got the baby in the bag?' I asked her.

'No,' she said, 'It's much too cold.'

I closed the door, saying, 'I'll tell Mother you called'; she knocked again and, laughing, walked past me, saying, 'I think your Mother would like to see me.'

I couldn't understand this but she stayed with Mother for a long time. Then I heard a baby cry; she must have brought the baby in the bag after all. I remember thinking that adults were very mysterious creatures sometimes. Jenny, as she was called, was so tiny, with lots of black hair and a funny screwed-up face. I thought she was beautiful. She wasn't a very happy baby and my job was to rock her to sleep. We were now four children, and what a tight squeeze it was in that tiny house! Why did we have to stay there?

I could see by the look on my parents' faces that things were not going too well, and as the days passed we were struggling to survive. Things went from bad to worse.

Early one morning I was wakened and told to get up and dress. It was still dark outside and very cold. Everyone was up and we were given tea and toast. The house was almost empty as our belongings were loaded in the truck. We were moving. I asked Mother if we were going back to the big house, but the look on her face told me, 'No.' I didn't ask any more questions – no one, it seemed, had any answers, or, if they had, it was obvious they were not going to tell me. I was urged to hurry up as John and I were to travel with Dad in the truck while Mother, with Dorothy and Jenny, was to travel by train. I wasn't sad to leave that terraced

7

house as there were no happy memories for me there.

John and I sat in the cabin of the truck with Dad. I noticed that he had a grim look on his face and he didn't speak at all. I didn't know where we were going; dawn came and John and I watched the countryside as it flashed by. At one stage, Dad must have been sleepy because we missed the bend in the road and we went into a ditch. We were jolted but not hurt. Dad checked the truck but didn't notice that a box, which contained important papers, had slipped off the back and apparently rolled into the hedge. It was never found, or perhaps I should say we weren't contacted to say that it had been found. I thought of Mother, Dorothy and Jenny and wondered how they were getting on – a train journey sounded very exciting to me.

We arrived at a town called Burton in the Midlands. Dad drove along a street lined with tired-looking houses. Stopping at one, he said, 'Here we are.' The front door led off the street and there was no garden. Dad said we would be sharing with another family. Apparently, we were to have three rooms, and the attic was to be our bedroom.

Mother arrived sometime later. She was very tired as Jenny had been fretful, and I could tell by looking at Dorothy that it had been no picnic. She wasn't impressed with our new accommodation – who would be? It was dreadful. We helped to unpack and it was a tight squeeze to fit everything in. I noticed that some of the good pieces of furniture were missing.

We had to make the best of the situation, but bed-time was a real hassle. To go to bed, we had to pass through our landlady's room, then climb wooden stairs to the attic. We always knocked on her door before going in, and we hoped that she wouldn't be in bed. I never got to know the man of the house, because sometimes there was a different man in bed with her. This puzzled me.

We were usually sent to bed early and it was a long night. There wasn't a light, just a very small window in the roof. We didn't have books, but if we had had, we wouldn't have been able to read them. I always told stories which I made up, and what rubbish they were! My characters were Laurel and Hardy, who were very popular at that time. I would drone on, stopping every now and then to ask if they were asleep; if I got no answer, I would turn over to sleep, otherwise I would continue.

Once again we were enrolled in the local school, and we settled down fairly well. I had always been subject to colds and this developed into bronchitis, which did interrupt my schooling.

CHAPTER 4

Dad lost heart. He had to sell the truck because there was no way that he could start up his business. We desperately needed the money, but this lasted only a short time; at least it was sufficient to feed us. He looked for work but he had no qualifications, only a good education. There were other families in the same situation so that when a job was advertised, there were many applicants. He didn't have a hope. Eventually, we existed on hand-outs and hand-me downs.

I was told that there was a world-wide depression, which was the basic cause of most families suffering hardships. This was wide-spread throughout the country. Not understanding the reason for this, I could only hope it would get better very soon. This miserable situation was taking its toll and we couldn't carry on like this. To me, a small child, it seemed that the world had turned upside down and we were going nowhere.

Mother's temper didn't improve. We did our best to please her, I know Dad did his best, but how could he work if there wasn't work to be had? After a few weeks, once again we were to move, and this time to a small town called Tutbury. Fortunately, it wasn't so far away but once again we were to share a house, which was situated in the main street. In no time at all our meagre belongings were unpacked.

It didn't take very long to settle in. The following day Dorothy was told to change the pillowcases but she emptied the ticks as well. Why she did this I don't really know but there were feathers everywhere. Was Mother cross! That was an understatement and in the heat of the moment, she told John and me to get out of the way. 'Go to school,' she said. Never brave enough to disobey, that was what we did. The boys' school was nearby. We had seen it so I took John's hand and we went in the gate. There were boys everywhere and John looked so small, although he was nearly nine years old. I told him to remember the date of his birthday and left him. I turned round to watch him; he was crying and boys were milling round him.

I went up the hill to the girls' school – it was a winding footpath and I walked slowly. Like the boys' school, there were girls everywhere. I stood alone. A bell rang and the girls rushed to get in line, but I stood where I was, tears running down my cheeks. One of the teachers saw me and, taking me by the hand, she led me into one of the classrooms. Before she was able to say anything, I blurted out that I was nearly eleven and that my birthday was in October.

She looked at me and said, 'Where's your mother?'

'Oh, she's busy,' I said. 'We've only just moved here.'

I was given a sheet of paper to do some spelling and adding up, then I was put into grade four. It was a big room with lots of girls, and they all looked at me when I was taken in.

At lunchtime I hurried home and John was already there. Mother said she wondered where we had got to, and that we should have said we were going to school; in any case, she did really tell us to go. I don't think she was too worried, she had other things on her mind. Dorothy had received a belting and had spent the morning picking up the feathers. She still had some in her hair. She was always in trouble.

It was a good school and I soon made friends. The infants' school was at the top of the playground and some had to stay over the lunch period. I was given the job of seeing that their faces were washed and hair brushed before school resumed. Occasionally, there was an accident in their knickers and I didn't like that job very much.

John said that the teacher had told him that he was too young for the big school, but that he would see how he got on. John liked the school and hoped that he would be able to stay. He did, and plodded on quite happily, but he wasn't an outstanding scholar.

Once a year was a 'Parents' Day'. It was an exciting day because parents were invited to see the school and their child's work. I was pleased that Mother was able to come because I had been chosen to recite a poem called 'The Glory of the Garden' which had eight verses. I loved poetry and didn't find it difficult to learn. Maybe Grandfather was partly responsible for this because he was always asking me to recite to him. Because I was small, I had to stand on a chair and when I looked at all those people, I began to stutter, but I did finish without a mistake.

11

Other girls played their part, including sister Dorothy. We showed Mother round the school and the work we were doing. We weren't clever, just plodders, but what a lovely afternoon it was! It remains in my memory.

A competition was held for writing with a number of the schools taking part. It was with great care that I copied the paragraph of twelve lines. Thin lines up, thick lines down, and good curves. There were five of us taking part and what a big thrill it was to be told I had won one of the prizes! It was good for the school also.

That school was an exciting and stimulating experience for me. I suppose I was a bit of a tom-boy, a dare-devil, as I had always loved to climb trees, just to hang upside down. The bars in the cloakroom were a great challenge, and I would climb up the pegs, then hang by my ankles. Could anything be better? It was great fun. I tempted other girls to do it, but most said it was dangerous, except Nellie Brown, who thought it was easy; so I dared her. She climbed up the pegs, then along the bar to hang by her knees; unfortunately, she fell, hitting her head on the tiled floor below. It did make a dreadful sound and I was very frightened. Someone went for the teacher, but not before I saw a huge swelling on her forehead, and she looked so ill. She was taken home and we didn't see her for a week.

When we assembled after this incident, the teacher, looking very hard at me, announced, 'I won't mention any name, but there is a girl in this class who will persist in swinging on the bars in the cloakroom. Now I'm giving fair warning that if she continues, she will be severely punished.'

I slid down in my desk, wishing to hide, but everyone knew that I was the culprit; however, within a week I was back swinging on the bars. It was an obsession – I just had to be upside down. I got caught and was given one hundred lines for my trouble. 'I must not swing on the bars in the cloakroom.' That was very hard work for me and it took a long time but no one was sympathetic, nevertheless, I was back on those bars whenever I could.

School was great; I used to wish there were no weekends, so that I could be there all the time. Once again it seemed that we were to move, but how happy I was to hear that it was not from the district, so we could still go to the same school.

CHAPTER 5

I can hear Ted busy in his workshop – he admits that he was a bit of a lad in his younger days. Children have no fear and in some situations are very lucky.

Among other things I was always attracted to fire; there was so much in a flame, and striking a match was very exciting for me. I did this whenever I had a chance. Firstly, there was a sudden sizzling noise when the match was struck, then I would watch as the flame crept along the small stick right to the end. The beginning of the match would burn black, then turn upwards, just like a horse's tail. I saw so many colours in that little flame; it didn't last long enough. I was fascinated.

Mother did catch me one time and warned me. How stupid I was not to heed that warning!

When I did get caught the next time, Mother didn't waste words, but got a sheet of newspaper, lit it with a match and held my fingers in the flame.

I screamed!

How could she do this to me? It was so painful but she always meant what she said. My fingers blistered and I couldn't use them for some time.

At school I was asked what had happened, but said that it was my own fault. Mother always expected obedience and to disobey was to be punished. I believe Mother received a letter from school stating that it was a cruel thing she had done, and that she was lucky not to be taken to court. My fingers healed well and nothing more was said, but I never played with matches again. Realising what fire could do, I have feared fire ever since.

I enjoyed reading, providing I could choose my own books. We had a good selection at school but unfortunately we were not allowed to take

13

any home. However, sometimes they were handed to us, and I was given *The Tale of Two Cities*, by Charles Dickens. I didn't like the look of it as it had very small print and looked very boring indeed. After a few days I handed it back, saying that I had read it. My teacher looked at me and said, 'Really, you've done very well,' then she gave me a sheet of paper saying, 'It's a long time since I read that book. Perhaps you could write a little about the story and what you thought of it.' She knew I hadn't read it. I tried hard, but I don't believe I ever read it.

Each month the school was visited by the school nurse who would check us over and inspect our hair. She found that I had lice and lots of nits. She also said that I was very thin and asked if I ate my meals. I would like to have told her that I always ate what I was given, but that there was never enough – I always had room for more. I told her that I was going to be a nurse one day. She just smiled, then gave me a note to give to Mother. Mother wasn't impressed, and I believe she was blamed for my having a dirty head. There was no nonsense about Mother and with the scissors she cut off all my hair. Next day I went to school wearing a cloth cap, and everyone knew that I had had a dirty head so they didn't want to play with me. I was so miserable I didn't want to go to school. At night I prayed that my hair would grow quickly.

Another baby arrived when I was twelve years old and I remember wondering why we had to have so many babies – surely they could go to other people! I knew there would be more work for me to do – babies made so much washing – and another thing, the food would have to stretch further.

We were now seven and very over-crowded; the rooms were much too small, so we moved to just outside Tutbury, but we still had to share the house. By this time I had accepted that we would not be going back to the big house. I often wondered who was living there and could only hope that they were as happy as I had been.

The house we moved into stood alone in a big garden, surrounded by trees and shrubs. We did have a little further to go to school, but that didn't worry us. Our landlady and her husband, Mr and Mrs Cole, were very nice people. They had two adult children who were living away from home. There was a lot more room and we soon unpacked and settled in.

Dad got a job cleaning bricks; I thought what a horrible job that was, but he was pleased and said it was better than nothing. He had to cycle there as it was some distance away. The pay was small, but I never heard him complain.

There was a soup kitchen near the school which was open twice a week. I always had two bowls – it was a welcome treat, especially on a cold day. The fat blobs floating on top didn't deter us; we tried to make them sink, but eventually we swallowed them.

When Tom, our last baby, was fifteen months old, we had another baby, a boy; we called him Sam. I used to look at him and say, 'Why did you have to come to our house, we can't afford you?' Then I realised that it wasn't his fault.

Dad worked hard and Mother did her best to make the food go round. John was doing odd jobs for Mrs Cole, for which he was paid. One morning John was washing his face at the sink and I don't know what happened – he wasn't a cheeky boy, but he must have said something that upset Mother because she raised her hand to slap him. He ducked and caught his head on the tap; it was a big cut, and bled a great deal. I thought he would have to go to the hospital to have it stitched, but mother just shook pepper on it – she had great faith in pepper. I really believe she was sorry that that had happened because she gave him a hug – a rare thing in our house. The cut healed well.

Mother's temper didn't improve – I kept out of her way when she was cross!

When Sam was six weeks old, Mother broke her leg. She was putting clothes on the line and fell over the clothes prop. She was very distressed and was taken to hospital. Mrs Cole offered to care for Sam, which was a relief for Dad, because he had to keep working.

We older children could manage; we were very self sufficient. Unfortunately, we weren't able to visit Mother very often; I always wanted to go as I wanted to watch the nurses. I would be a nurse one day – I was sure of that. Dad went when he could. Sam thrived under Mrs Cole's care – she loved him.

Dorothy did the cooking on the wood stove, but always forgot to keep it stoked. Often she would relight it, forgetting that there was something in the oven. Her pastry, I remember, went through this process and we couldn't eat it – it was too hard – but Dad, the Trojan that he was, said it was delicious.

15

Friday night was bath night. The old tin bath was brought up from the shed and placed in front of the stove. It was filled with water that was heated in the copper. John was always the last in, and the water was so mucky for him. After the bath we were given a dose of brimstone and treacle – I wasn't sure what for; maybe it was for the bowels. It wasn't unpleasant to take but we didn't have any trouble going to the toilet to do what was called No 2. Mother was in hospital for a long time. She had been diagnosed as having a compound fracture of her leg, which was much more severe than a simple fracture.

On one occasion when I was taken to visit, I could see that she was wanting to be home. She had a plaster cast on her leg, from the ankle to well above the knee. A large cage covered this to keep off the bedclothes.

As I sat by her bedside, I was fascinated and interested in all that was going on. I would have loved to have asked questions, but I knew that I couldn't. When Mother did eventually come home Sam was six months old, a chubby, healthy and happy little baby.

It was then I heard that we'd been offered a cottage on a nearby farm estate. My parents grabbed it, so once again we were to move but only a short distance.

CHAPTER 6

There were two cottages, semi-detached. They were in the middle of a field, surrounded by a wooden fence which kept out the animals. We learned that they were over one hundred years old, and built of solid brick, with that old-world charm.

Inside was a different story. There were two rooms on the ground floor. One room, the main one, was long and had a red brick floor with the wood stove at one end. The pieces of furniture that we owned fitted in well, with the old kitchen table in the middle. On this stood the paraffin lamp – our only means of light. The smaller room had the copper. Upstairs there were three bedrooms, and they had concrete floors which were very cold. Except for the beds and a chest of drawers, there was little else, certainly no carpet to put on the floor. The windows were very small and there were no curtains. Heading up the stairs were eight steep steps.

We were happy there. Without a landlady to think about, we could sing, shout, make a lot of noise, the cows weren't worried, and we had a big garden. What a prize that was! Dad was so pleased. Very soon it was prepared for planting. Round the garden were fruit trees – pears, apples, plums and a damson tree. The farmer wanted the damsons, as his wife made jam with them.

A young couple lived next door but as they were at work all day, we saw very little of them. They didn't stay long and the cottage was taken over by a family of four children, with whom we were to get on very well.

John had many responsibilities; he had to light the copper on Monday morning because it was wash day and for Friday evening bath night. To get water we had to pump it. The pump was outside – it was a horrible thing to use, especially in the winter, and sometimes it would take a long time for the water to flow. Another of John's responsibilities was to

17

black-lead the stove. He hated doing this and always got more on his face than on the stove. I had to scrub that red brick floor – it seemed huge and took ages. These chores were done every Friday evening.

Round our two decanters were silver tags, 'whisky' and 'gin'. They had to shine so that we could see our faces in them. They were family heirlooms from the big house and had been carefully carried with us on each of our moves. How lovely it would have been to be able to take them back to the big house!

Dad's favourite flowers were asters and when he was able, he planted lots. The garden thrived and we had plenty of vegetables. Sad to say, Dad didn't make cucumber frames – that episode in my life was just a dream.

We were a healthy bunch of children; it was so easy to pull up a carrot, turnip or swede to munch on. Sweets were never seen in our house, but we did pinch some cocoa and mixed it with sugar, which was very nice. We all did that so it didn't last long.

It was quite some time before we realised that Sam was not to live with us. He was such a lovely baby, but our former landlady didn't wish to part with him. She begged to be able to keep him, she loved him so much and he had filled a void in their lives. I believe he did stay with us for a few days but he wasn't happy, so he went back to them. Once again I asked why, but there were no answers. I was told that I was a sticky beak. I had to take it for granted that Mother and Dad knew what they were doing, as they thought he would have a better future with his foster parents. We lost touch, and could only hope that he was happy. It was later, when Mother and Dad died, that Dorothy, who had never forgiven them for parting with Sam, searched for him. This wasn't difficult, as he wasn't too far away. Apparently he had heard the request on the wireless and they were able to meet. It was a lovely reunion, and the likeness to Grandfather was amazing, even to having a grey beard.

Life hadn't been easy for him as both his foster parents had been crippled with arthritis and he had had to care for them. He must have been excited and pleased to have been 'found', as it were. He knew he had a family somewhere but wasn't told. Sam and Dorothy are very close now and visit when possible; he does have a wife and family.

When on a trip to England later I was able to visit. What a big thrill that was! But my thoughts have jumped the years – if one lives long enough, there is so much to think about, time tends to telescope. *Which reminds me – it is nearly lunch time and Ted will be getting hungry. Despite his age he still has a healthy appetite and I always have a meal ready for him.*

The house was surrounded by fields and there were cows, and sometimes the bull was with them. What a massive brute he was, and I didn't like the look in his eyes. We were apprehensive at first and always kept our distance, but very soon we overcame this. Sometimes they would come close to the fence, and we learned very quickly to keep the gate closed. We could see how eager they were to sample our vegetables, which must have looked very appetizing to them.

One Saturday a young farm hand was walking a horse in the field, and every now and then he would try to mount it. Dad watched for a while from the fence, then asked the young fellow what he was trying to do. He got a surly reply, then he turned to go. I could see that Dad was getting annoyed, and wanted to give him a lecture on how to handle horses, but instead he said, 'Let me ride him.' The young fellow reluctantly handed over the reins, saying, 'Don't blame me if you get hurt.' Dad was in his element, and after speaking to the horse in soothing tones, he climbed on its back. The horse pranced about for a short time, but Dad had full control – he knew about horses.

Suddenly, they took off; what a lovely sight! With Dad's jacket billowing behind, they disappeared across the field. It was about fifteen minutes later that they returned, a tired horse and a jubilant Dad; he was absolutely breathless with pleasure. He helped me up to sit on its back.

Remembering Tommy and Bessie, I asked if I could give it a lump of sugar. I was thinking again of the big house. Dad said I could give it an apple. If the young fellow was pleased, he didn't say, but climbed on its back and trotted away.

One very warm day there was a commotion at the near-by river, and we ran down to see what it was all about. A horse had fallen in and was distressed and frightened, as it had got stuck in the mud. I wanted to go to it, and tears ran down my face as I watched the men get it out. It took at least an hour, and thank goodness the horse was all right. It had been worked all day in the field without a drink and, on seeing the water, had rushed in. How could anyone be so cruel? I do hope the farmer who owned the farm read the riot act to whoever was responsible.

We loved helping round the farm and would round up the cows for milking. The old farm dog knew the drill; he would give a few barks and amble behind them. I had a favourite cow I named 'Tich' and she would come to me when I called. With my arm across her shoulder, we would walk to the farm. Sometimes I was allowed to milk her and what a big thrill that was!

John and I did some weeding in the garden for the farmer's wife. John wasn't impressed when we weren't paid; as he said, 'She expected a lot done for nothing.' Occasionally, we were given a piece of treacle tart and I liked that.

One Saturday morning, as we were doing nothing in particular, we were asked to feed the bull which was in his stall. We were told, 'Just take in this bowl of grass and tip it into his trough.' It sounded easy enough. I opened the door just a little; perhaps the bull was curious as to what was happening, or maybe he wanted to get at the grass. He pushed the door and I couldn't hold it; John rushed to help and together we tried to shut the door. I could see that the bull was winning so I left John to run and hide, but he followed me very fast. Sensing freedom, the bull came out with a roar. Two farmhands with sticks tried to coax it back, but the bull proved difficult and ran round the yard. It was very excited, and it took some time to calm it down and lead it back to the stall. That chore was not for us – we were never asked to do it again.

Jenny was a petite little girl who was always getting into mischief. She loved to help round up the cows, she didn't understand fear, and had been told many times not to go in the field if the bull were with the cows. It was no surprise one day to see her following the cows. She was tiny and hard to see, and was some distance from our fence. When we saw her, the bull had also spotted her and was pawing the ground. John and I were horrified; we yelled but she took no notice. The bull charged but she didn't move, just stood still. Within a few feet of her it stopped and after what seemed hours it turned away. Jenny ran towards us; she just said, 'He was a nice old cow and I told him so.'

Carting in the hay was a very busy time for the farmers, and the weather played a big part. However, we thought it great fun. The tractor would go up and down the field cutting the hay, which was tied in sheaves. We followed behind to prop them up to form pyramids – this was called 'stooking'. It was a demanding job, dusty and back-breaking.

The short stalks left behind were very brittle and scratched our legs. We couldn't afford socks. The sheaves were left to dry, then carted in. There were always two four-wheeled wagons on the go, which were pulled by horses – great lumbering giants, but so gentle. My job was to lead the horse to the field, then bring it back with a load of hay. To the horse I must have looked a midget; in fact, I doubt if he saw me at all, but only heard my voice as I talked to him. Being small made no difference to me – I was so full of confidence.

One day I was on top of the stack; this was fun, but I slipped, falling between the horse and the shaft. Not a movement did that horse make as I crawled from between his legs! I had cut my hand as I had fallen. It was a big gash. The farmer's wife put a pad on it, and I went home. I thought it might have to have stitches, and I remembered the time when, falling through the cucumber frame, I had cut my foot very badly – that was stitched and it was very painful. Mother looked at it but she didn't get hassled, just shook pepper on it, then bandaged it. Her faith in pepper must have been justified as the cut healed well.

The chickens roamed freely at the farm and sometimes we found eggs in the most unusual places. We were able to take some home – a rare treat – but some must have been lying around for a long time, as we found out when we broke the shell and the smell hit us.

Half a pint of milk was our daily ration, which we got from the farm, in a tin can; we couldn't afford any more. Milk wasn't on the menu for us older ones.

At school everyone talked about Shrove Tuesday. Apparently, pancakes were made on that day but they would have been a luxury for us. Nevertheless, as Mother and Dad were out, John and I decided to make some but Dorothy wasn't interested. We searched the cupboard, but only found flour and sugar. There wasn't any fat, but John found a small jar of goose-grease so we decided to use that. After mixing the flour and sugar with water, it didn't look too bad. Putting some of the goose-grease in the pan, we spooned in the batter. They browned beautifully, we turned them over, they looked very good. Then we tasted them but they were so horrible that we couldn't eat them and they were thrown out. Mother said afterwards that goose-grease was a special ointment to rub on the chest when we had a cough or a cold.

How we loved mushrooms! They were free so we were able to have our fill without being checked. When they were in season I would go with Dad to tramp the fields in the early hours of the morning – we knew where to get them. Any excess we took to the greengrocer who would sell them, and we would be given a small percentage of the money. This was a means of supplementing our income.

One Saturday afternoon while playing, we heard a roar and, looking up, realised our chimney was on fire. My first thought was to hide. Sparks were thrown out and it looked very frightening as soot fell in heaps in the sitting room. I thought the house would burn down – I knew what fire could do. I watched fearfully, thinking maybe we would have to move again, and perhaps once again to have a landlady. It couldn't bear thinking about. Dad was working at the time but Mother, her usual calm self in an emergency, just watched it, saying that it would burn itself out. Then she added, 'The chimney needed sweeping anyway.' It did burn itself out. John wasn't impressed as he had to clean up the mess. Dad spread the soot on the garden when he came home, and all was well. The stove cooked so much better and there wasn't any smoke billowing into the room.

Ours was a very busy house; the time seemed to fly, and we were growing up fast.

CHAPTER 7

Our cottage was called 'Rabbit Pit Cottage' the reason being that it was surrounded by rabbit warrens. Dad was to curse these many times, especially the big ones near the front. To get to the road, we could go round by the drive which led from the farm, but this was a long way. We always decided to go across the field, then hop over the gate – it was much shorter.

I could never understand why Dad always found himself at the bottom of the big rabbit warren. When it was foggy, he did have an excuse. It was a wonder that he didn't hurt himself, but he had had to carry his bike as he climbed out. If only rabbits could talk, what stories they could tell! I don't believe I ever heard Dad swear, but he must have had his own dictionary because he did say some funny words. On foggy evenings Mother would put the lamp in the window but, of course, we couldn't see it. I always wondered why she did it. I suppose she thought in some small way she was helping.

Rabbit was always on the menu, which was not surprising really; anyway, we couldn't afford red meat. Mother did wonders when cooking them. I hated seeing them killed and didn't like the smell either, but we thrived on them. Dad brought a baby one home one day and he gave it to me. I asked him what had happened to its mother, but he said he didn't know. I gave it lots of cuddles, and took it to bed with me, as I didn't want it to be cold. I woke next morning to find it lying dead beside me. Dad said not to worry as it was probably missing its mother and wouldn't have survived anyway. I buried it in the garden.

We were given a small dog, a bitser; he had a black and white body, with white paws. We named him Victor and what a lovely nature he had. We loved him very much and I believe he thought he was human. He had lots of fun chasing rabbits but they were too quick for him – I don't remember him actually catching one. Dad trained him to meet us from school and with his lead attached he would cross the field where he would patiently wait at the gate. He was so clever and when it was foggy he never faulted, always taking us straight home.

About this time Mother took to going out every Saturday evening. She would dress in her best to catch the bus to town and we wouldn't see her until the following morning.

Dad would wait up for her as she was very inebriated on many occasions and he would have to help her across the field. We couldn't understand this situation – how could she afford this? There wasn't anything we could do; her temper didn't improve and we kept out of her way.

I believe she continued her life in this fashion until she died. I've always been sad about this; life was very difficult for her, for both of them, after the big house. She was unhappy, disillusioned. I don't know how Dad felt – he never said. He wasn't the domestic type and I'm sure he found coping with children extremely difficult.

But what a life he had! With no qualifications except a good education, it wasn't a happy life for him. His business failed after we left the big house and no matter how he tried, he couldn't get back on his feet. He had never really worked hard in his youth and I believe before marriage he was a gay young man, a happy bachelor.

I wondered why he just walked out of the big house; after caring for grandfather he should have been compensated, but he got nothing. I thought he got on well with his family; at least, it appeared so. Nevertheless, I didn't hear him complain and he plodded on. I did hear later that the family had searched for him. I don't believe Mother was too popular with the family. She was seventeen years younger than Dad and he came from a good home and was popular with the opposite sex. Dad did his best, they both did, but the odd jobs he got were very degrading. When employed cleaning bricks, he would sit for hours chipping off the cement then stacking them. His wages were poor and not sufficient to pay bills.

One day he wasn't there and we were told that he was in jail. I was horrified – people like my Dad didn't go to jail. I was puzzled as to why, then I heard the rates hadn't been paid and that was the reason. I couldn't understand that; how could he pay the rates if he were in jail? While there, apparently he sewed mail bags. Sad to say he went to jail twice and during that time we lived on hand-outs, hand-me-downs and there was the soup kitchen.

Dad never raised his voice; though I'm sure he must have, I didn't hear him. Maybe he talked to the plants in the garden – he spent as much time as possible there. He got very tired and slept as soon as he sat in his armchair. We would put small things on his head, then giggle when his head slipped and fell forward. Poor Dad took it all in good part.

I don't remember Mother and Dad going out together, and there was only one occasion when Dad went to a club. He returned home drunk, flopped on his chair and slept and stayed there all night. That never happened again.

Sometimes he would tell us stories of what he did when he was single. He loved ice-skating and was very good at it; he could have become a professional. I remember seeing skates in the shed. One day he said he was skating on the river; there were other skaters as well, and a small child slid in front of him. Dad knew he couldn't stop or avoid hitting the child, so he bent down, picked him up and took him with him. The child thought it great fun, but Dad was shaken; it would have been a disastrous situation.

He also told us how he would go shooting with his gun dogs, to shoot pheasants. Apparently his life was full before marriage but it was to become so very crowded and stressful after his father's death. What a change for him!

Sunday morning was a busy time when Dorothy and Mother would do the usual jobs. Dorothy always had to help; she didn't have much freedom. John and I were told to take the two little ones and to get out of the way, which we were quite happy to do.

We had a big pram and we would put Jenny and Tom in it. It was inclined to tip one end and Tom being the heavier of the two would sit the other end to balance it. John and I liked these walks; they were good fun and a great adventure. It was on one of these walks one Sunday morning that we took a wrong turning and ahead of us was a bridge. It was very old but inviting and we trudged slowly on. It didn't feel very safe and there were large holes through which we could see the swirling waters below. It was difficult pushing the pram and trying to avoid these holes for the wheels kept getting caught between the rotten planks. Continuing very slowly we heard someone yelling. Looking towards the end of the bridge we saw a man dancing and waving his hands about. He frightened us somewhat and we turned to go back. He yelled more loudly still and beckoned us forward.

'Hurry up, can't you kids read? The bridge is dangerous and could collapse any time.'

We said we were sorry, we didn't see the notice, but that we had to get home for dinner.

'You'll have to go round, you can't go back across the bridge.'

Not sure where we were, we trudged on, taking turns to push the big pram. Tom and Jenny were getting restless; they probably needed their knickers changed. Eventually we found the path which would take us home, where we were reprimanded for being late. No one listened to our story, so we just ate our dinner.

Some Sunday mornings before breakfast we rode our bikes which were very old – I believe Dad picked them up from the tip and repaired them. Tom and Jenny always came with us; they sat on the carrier. We often went to the local swimming pool where I learnt to swim, but John wasn't fond of the water, he just played about.

Sunday mornings were adventure mornings for John and me. Often we would go on the common to play with the gipsies if they were there. They were allowed to stay for a short time. Some were very nice but others were rude and dirty. I suppose we looked grubby to them also. There were no fences round the common, which was a stretch of ground surrounded by a few trees, bushes and hedges. In season we were able to pick hazelnuts from these hedges.

The weather never deterred us – there was always somewhere to go and something to do. We made our own entertainment.

Our proud possession was a very old gramophone though we only had one record, 'Colonel Bogey', but we had lots of fun. We were opera stars, ballet dancers – you name it, we were it. We dressed in old curtains, socks, whatever we could find. The children from next door joined in, and we got to know them better. They were the Merrit family. There were four children – two boys and two girls; I don't know where they came from but they were friendly, which was a big plus when we were isolated in the middle of a field surrounded by a fence. The three eldest attended school, so we all walked together.

Mr Merrit appeared to have a good job; at least, he wasn't cleaning

26

bricks like my Dad. They had better furniture than we had and I was so envious. Mrs Merrit was very small and she didn't look well; she didn't speak much and I thought she was unhappy. Like most mothers she was always busy with the household chores.

One day I heard Mother telling Dad when he came home from work that as she was pegging out the washing, Mrs Merrit had rushed at her with a large carving knife, yelling, 'You're the devil, I've found you at last.' Mother got an awful fright and said it took some time to subdue her. Over a cup of tea she said they had talked about it but Mrs Merrit couldn't believe that she had done such a thing – there appeared no reason for the outburst, except that she had frequent headaches and got very tired. It was some time later in the early hours of the morning that the stillness was shattered by terrible screams coming from next door. Mother and Dad rushed round to find Mr Merrit holding his wife tightly. Apparently she had suddenly gone berserk and was trying to strangle her youngest child with a belt.

Her husband was in a dreadful state. Dad came back and told John and me to dress and fetch the doctor. It was 2.30 a.m. and very dark and it was a long way to walk. Nevertheless, putting Victor on a lead, we set off. We walked across the field, having full confidence in Victor.

Arriving at the doctor's house we knocked loudly. Poking his head out of an upper window, he asked, 'What do you want?' We explained what had happened. He grunted, he wasn't happy about being disturbed and said so. We waited while he dressed, which seemed ages. He didn't know us as it was only on a very rare occasion that we needed a doctor. He looked us over; well, we weren't very well clothed, but we were clean.

'You come with me,' he said, 'I can't take the dog in the car.'

John said nothing but I knew what he was thinking. He said, 'You go with the doctor – Victor and I will walk home.'

Sitting next to him in the car, I wanted to tell him that I was going to be a nurse when I was able, but he didn't speak and I sensed he wasn't too happy at the distance we had to travel. Parking the car at the roadside, we walked across the field. Thank goodness, it wasn't foggy but I did smile to myself at the thought that he might fall down a rabbit hole – wouldn't that shake him up! When I was a nurse I hoped I wouldn't meet surly doctors like him, but I did many times when I eventually became a State Registered Nurse. I asked myself why should they be different from us, we are entitled to be grumpy at times, but somehow I didn't expect this as a small child walking across the field to a sick woman.

All was quiet at home. Dad was concerned about John and Victor walking home alone so I said I would look out for them. The doctor was with Mrs Merrit a long time. He said that he was going to send an ambulance when he got back to his surgery; apparently Mrs Merrit was a very sick woman, so he had given her a sedative and she was sleeping. I took him back across the field and looked for John and Victor but I couldn't hear them and I certainly couldn't see them. I waited for a while and they arrived soon after; it had been a long walk, but then we did this walk twice a day to school. I gave John a big hug – we were very close.

There was no more sleep that night for us. I wanted to know what was the matter with Mrs Merrit, but as usual there were no answers to my questions. She died in hospital very soon after, so she must have been sicker than we thought. The family were very sad, especially the two younger children; they couldn't understand that they wouldn't see their mother again.

However, when anything goes wrong, especially something over which we have no control, children do adapt and accept the situation. It was so with them. The two eldest children took over the running of the house and Mother gave advice when she could. They did their best but it wasn't the same.

I felt sorry for Mr Merrit and as I loved my Dad, I felt he needed to be loved too. He went to work as usual but Friday evening would find him coming home very unsteady on his feet as he had been drinking. This continued regularly and I would look out for him so that I could help him home. He did his best for the children but they were a handful, unruly and disobedient; he must have been very lonely.

At times he would put his arm round me but I would shrug him off. This became constant so I avoided him, as I didn't like that. On one occasion he chased me round the kitchen table and when he caught me, he hugged me to him, breathing very hard. I was breathless too. Then he suggested a cuddle on the floor maybe, asking if I would like to lie with him for a little while as there was no one about. I struggled to get free, I didn't like what was happening and said so. He was very persistent, but when he did eventually let go of me, he was very red in the face. I was

28

puzzled about his actions, and frightened and I certainly wasn't happy about the situation; I just thought, what a silly man!

I didn't tell Mother and Dad about this but I made sure I wouldn't be alone with him again. I didn't avoid him, the attraction being that he always had a pot of potatoes boiling in their jackets on the stove. Oh, how I loved those. He never put his arm around me again, thank goodness. We were survivors, sharing our joys and sorrows.

Often gipsies camped on the nearby common and they would come round selling their wares – some were very nice and we would play with them.

One day, seeing Victor, they asked if they could have him. 'No!' we cried but they said, 'It's a pity, really, because you won't have him long.'

How would they know that? We said they were jealous and had put a curse on him but we hoped not. A few weeks later he sat patiently waiting for me to come home from school. I was late and he was so pleased to see me that he rushed across the road, a thing he had never done before, and he was run over by a car travelling very fast which didn't stop. I screamed, I picked him up and as I carried him home, he died in my arms.

Next day a policeman came to school to ask questions about Victor. Apparently my screams had caught the attention of the house up the road; also, the driver of the car, fearing his number had been taken, had reported the incident to the police station. He said he had run over a stray dog with no collar. This wasn't true; not only did Victor have a collar but his lead was attached to it. There were five very sad children for a long time. Dad missed him too but didn't say so, but I knew how he loved Victor. Later we were given another dog and I remember he was covered with fleas. We named him 'Sandy', but he never took Victor's place.

Life went on; our parents did their best for us but there were many families struggling to survive in difficult situations. The world-wide depression continued but, not understanding what that was all about, I didn't worry about it. As we grew so did our appetites and we always had room for more, but there was none. We didn't eat bought meat until we were teenagers but there was always rabbit. Ugh!

CHAPTER 8

Being the first born of the family, a lot was expected of Dorothy. As she got older it was obvious that she and Mother didn't get on well together. She always got things wrong and she did get a lot of beatings. I believe she enjoyed school; she never said, but she did remark that she didn't like the weekends. Although we lived together for so many years, she didn't feature very much in my life. Her cooking improved as she matured and if given the right ingredients, she would have made an excellent cook. Like me, she was no academic but plodded through the lessons. She never said that there was anything special that she wished to do when she grew up.

She left school at the age of fourteen. She was a very attractive girl and I wondered if this were the reason she and Mother didn't get on. Did Mother sense competition? Dorothy always wanted to please and she would end up making a nuisance of herself. Nevertheless, she was packed off to work as a domestic in a private house. She was out of Mother's hair and for a while all seemed well. Then one day we were told that she was in hospital as she had attempted to take her own life. I couldn't believe this but as the story unfolded, I was very sad and sorry for her. Apparently, her employer had been abusing her for some time, then she realised that she was pregnant. Her employer gave her pills to take. His wife was very ill and he was worried as to how this problem would affect her if she heard about it. The pills didn't work.

Mother confronted Dorothy's employer, but he denied everything. She threatened to take him to court. However, realising the position he held and that it was his word against Dorothy's, Mother knew that it was hopeless and would be too costly so she had to let the matter drop.

Dorothy got better but for a while it was touch and go. Fortunately, she lost the baby.

After being home for a short time she again went into domestic service. She wasn't happy but she had no choice and had to make the best of it. Eventually, she was able to get a position as a dining room maid, which suited her very well. It was at the local hospital, where I was to catch up with her later.

We always weathered the storms as they surfaced and there were many, but one was particularly traumatic. I was thirteen years old when one evening Mother slipped on a banana skin and fractured her skull. She had been drinking but not to excess, and was admitted to hospital unconscious.

We carried on, we were a healthy bunch of children and didn't see a doctor very often. We were self-sufficient, able to do the household chores and shopping; we were well trained. Mother didn't wait on us, but encouraged us to look after ourselves as soon as we were able.

In the meantime Dad developed a nasty cold and a persistent cough. He was out all day in all weathers cleaning bricks, and he certainly didn't have sufficient warm clothing. He looked ill and I asked the doctor to see him. On examination he shook his head, saying that Dad was very ill and would have to go into hospital. The doctor would send the ambulance for him. Poor Dad, I believe he worried about us, and while we waited I gave him a wash all over, then shaved him with an open razor. He accepted both but looked apprehensive when I waved the razor; however, I didn't find it difficult. I'm sure he felt much more comfortable when I had finished.

John, only eleven years, was very good and he was always ready to help. There was much to do with the younger children, especially now with both our parents in hospital. Fortunately, they were attending school. Dad was on the danger list for some time; in fact, John was told that he wouldn't recover. Mother progressed slowly and when told about Dad, she said, 'He'll be all right.' She was always calm in an emergency. Would I have this calm outlook when I became a nurse? I hoped so. Both were in hospital for some time.

One morning when making porridge for breakfast I spilt some on my foot. It was very painful and a large blister formed. I took Jenny and Sam to school, was excused myself, then went to hospital to visit Mother and Dad. Mother looked concerned when she saw me hobbling down the ward. I told her what had happened. A nurse took me to a small room where she took off the bandage saying, 'Tut tut.' She changed the

31

dressing daily and it soon healed. How I loved the smell of the hospital! I could watch the nurses all day as they went about their duties. I knew that I would be a nurse one day – it couldn't come soon enough for me.

John coped well with his responsibilities; he didn't have much of a boyhood. Friends helped a lot during this time and our school teachers, knowing of our problems, were understanding.

When visiting Mother, I noticed that a young boy regularly visited his mother in the next bed. He was older than I and we got to know one another quite well. It was the first time I had thought about boys. I had heard silly rumours about how babies were formed but didn't believe them; as far as I was concerned, babies just turned up or they were found under a cabbage leaf. Men and women just got together to look after them. How immature I was in that side of life! I thought of Mr Merrit, and realised what his intentions had been. It couldn't bear thinking about.

This boy was rather nice and I wanted to be nearer to him; I got a tickle in my tummy when I looked at him. He told me that he hoped to be a policeman one day and that he had been studying hard. His father had died two years before and his mother was very frail. She had a bone disease in her foot. It wasn't going to be easy for him.

I would have liked to continue the friendship but this wasn't possible. Sitting by his mother's bed, we talked a lot. I said I hoped that he would be able to do what he wished and that I was sure he would make a very good policeman. My parents were to be discharged the following day. He kissed me on the cheek and said goodbye.

Mother soon resorted to her old way of life – she was a lucky woman, recovering as she did with no side effects. In one of her lighter moods she told me of her own mother. I was surprised to hear that I had been named after her. For years she had been a midwife and would travel round in a pony and trap with her little terrier for company. This little dog would patiently wait until Gran was finished. As a midwife she was very popular, and I was really thrilled to be told that she had delivered John and me. One of her outstanding features was the large starched white apron that she always wore.

I loved hearing about this and I wanted more, but for Mother to talk about her past was unusual – she had to be in the right frame of mind. I knew then that I was going to be like my Gran.

Dad went back to work cleaning bricks but he didn't look well and I was sad for him.

The back door opens and Ted comes in. 'Enjoying a rest? The sun is quite warm.' He's wearing well, I think, there's no doubt he's a busy bee, always finding something to do, what a help it would be if he could cook but he can't do everything.

'Have you finished the chair?' I ask him.

'Almost,' he says.

How proud he is, the chair, a very old rocking chair, was in a very bad state of repair; his wood-turning is superb. He's truly married to his woodwork. In a way I suppose this is natural as he is a product of three generations of woodworkers: wheelwrights and coach builders.

My thoughts return to the past.

CHAPTER 9

How could this be!!! At fourteen years of age I had to leave school. I didn't want to but had no choice. I was considered grown up and my school days were over. It was almost a tragedy. What happy days they had been!

My school report was satisfactory; I had plodded on. I had learnt that the Battle of Hastings was in 1066 and that in 1215 the Magna Carta was signed – that was history! As for geography, well, at least I could find my country on the map. Thinking back on my last days of school, I wondered what the future held for me. But I had plans, big plans. One thing that I was sure of was that I would soon be out in the work-force, no doubt about that. I would be expected to contribute towards household expenses.

I stood in front of the headmistress and thought how kind and helpful she had been. I had been given a prize for good conduct, a box of paints – how excited I was! I loved drawing and painting but had had very little time to indulge in it.

There were five other students leaving at the same time and as she looked at us, she smiled and wished us a happy future. I told her I would be a nurse one day. She had heard this before, many times but her answer didn't dampen my spirits – she didn't think I could possibly make the grade. Thanking her, I wished her 'goodbye'. I had my own idea – I would make it.

There were no idle hands in our house and very soon I was bundled into domestic service. It was very strange. I was away from home for the first time, but was soon put to work and there wasn't time to dream. My lady boss was a saleswoman selling vacuum cleaners door to door. I don't know if she was successful, but at the time I did think they would have saved a lot of work.

Her husband had an office job somewhere. I avoided him when

possible as he was always wanting to fondle me; he said I was a nice young girl. I was considered an adult, but I was young at heart and very naive.

There were three schoolchildren and when they were home they were my responsibility. It was a big house, but I was well trained to get on with the job. My bedroom was in the attic with just the bare necessities. I worked long hours and wasn't over fed.

After I had been there for six weeks Mother arrived. Why hadn't I sent money home? She wasn't impressed when I said I hadn't been paid. Questions were asked and Mother was told that I would be paid the following week.

'That isn't good enough,' said Mother crossly, then to me, 'Emily, pack your case; you're coming home.'

I was never paid for those six weeks, but I was pleased to be leaving the place – even home was a welcome sight. There was fresh air, the freedom, Dad's vegetable garden and I believe Tich the cow recognised me when I called her. It seemed that I had been away years. There was a lot to be said for living in the country, especially on a farm estate.

I was home for a short while. My next job was in a factory, I had to paint drink crates and was paid 1s.3d. a hundred. I cycled the five miles to work, and had to be there to start work at six o'clock. We finished at six in the evening. It was long hours, a smelly dirty job and I hated it. I was very sick the first week and had a nasty cough and lost my appetite. I accepted this and eventually got used to the smell of paint everywhere.

The benches were small and we worked two to a bench. I was popular, as being left handed made the work that much easier and much more comfortable than with two right handed people. They were a good crowd in the workshop and the foreman was a jovial fellow, always telling jokes. We were on piece-work which meant that if we were slow we wouldn't earn very much! As the boxes were painted they were stacked one on top of the other and left to dry. Being small, this wasn't easy for me.

The days were long but it was the same for everyone. Mother bought me a new bike on hire purchase. She always took my pay packet and gave a little back for pocket money.

When Mother's birthday was coming up I decided to keep a little money from my pay and buy her a present. Deciding on a tea set with a willow pattern, I put it on the layby. On her birthday I was so pleased to give it to her, but her reaction startled me. She accused me of stealing and I was given a belting. I just didn't understand why Mother could be so aggressive, but I wouldn't and didn't do it again. I did hear later that she prized that tea-set, always telling how Emily had saved to buy it for her. When she died there apparently was one piece left! I didn't want it.

John joined me in the factory. I believe he was to be an apprentice to the wood trade. He did very well, and was liked by his fellow workers. He never completed his apprenticeship, as war was imminent, and he joined the army, which I thought was very unfortunate.

Cycling to work one foggy morning I didn't see the car until I was almost on top of it. I swerved and my pedal scraped along the side. It made a nasty sound but I didn't stop. Finding that I couldn't put my foot on the pedal, I found it had been pulled back. Not being able to ride the bike like that, I had to walk. At work one of the fellows fixed it for me. I didn't tell Dad as he would have said that I was careless and must always be on the lookout, especially in the fog.

In the meantime my sister was established as a dining room maid at the local hospital. She enjoyed her work and was very happy. One day she told me there was a vacancy; I applied, and got the job. I couldn't believe it. At last I was in a hospital, if only as a domestic. I was only 16½ years old – there was still time to achieve my ambition.

No more cycling mile after mile: I was to live in and have my own room. With regular meals, who could complain? Certainly not I. What a big change, a different outlook, a different situation!

My duties were cleaning the bathrooms and toilets and what seemed to be miles and miles of corridors. The nurses had to dust their own rooms which were thoroughly cleaned once a month by another maid, whose job it was doing just that. None of this worried me, and my sister Dorothy being there too was a big advantage. Most of our wages were sent home but we were allowed to keep a little.

The home sister and tutor sister shared a small sitting room on my floor, and it was my responsibility to keep it clean and also to prepare morning and afternoon tea. Those two people were wonderful and always praised the work I did. I wanted to please and did take my menial tasks seriously.

One afternoon when I took in their tea they asked if I intended staying as a domestic.

'Oh no, when I'm old enough I'm going to be a nurse.'

Nothing more was said for a few weeks but I was counting the days to my eighteenth birthday which was when I was hoping to get into a hospital.

It was during afternoon tea that they called me in their sitting room.

'Sit down, Emily,' they said. 'Now where would you like to do your training?'

I didn't know, I just wanted to get into a hospital.

They suggested that I send for application forms from different hospitals. The replies were disappointing as I was considered too young for general training, the age limit being twenty-one. However, one application form I had sent for was for training at a sanatorium for tuberculosis. This one stated that as I was eighteen I could apply.

To say I was nonplussed reading the questions was an understatement. My spelling was appalling but the sisters understood; they answered the questions, and I copied them onto the application form. One question almost stumped us. It read, 'What is your present occupation?' Would they accept me if I said that I was a domestic? Oh no!! Domestics didn't become student nurses. I was well aware of the class distinction at that time.

It was suggested I just state, 'At home', so with fingers crossed, I popped the completed application form in the post.

Waiting for a reply seemed to take ages although it was only two weeks. I had to produce two references and a medical certificate and I could have a chance of being accepted. The sister tutor wrote one reference and for the other one I wrote to my headmistress at school. I would love to have seen her face when she read my request. She replied by return mail stating that she would be pleased to help me at any time.

When I told Mother and Dad, Dad was pleased for me, saying that it was what I had dreamed of, but Mother was not so optimistic, saying, 'You make your bed, you lie on it.' The letter arrived. I was accepted and requested to report to the sanatorium on New Year's Eve. The year was 1936 and I was eighteen years old.

When I handed in my resignation at the hospital where I was working, Matron was very surprised, saying that she thought I was happy there and enjoyed my work. I did not tell her of my future plans – just that I wanted a change. How lovely it would have been to tell her the truth but I was apprehensive, fearing that the matron at the sanatorium would find out that I had been a domestic. I couldn't risk that possibility.

Those dear hospital sisters gave me a pocket watch and wished me all the best as I said goodbye. I was to catch up with the sister tutor later. She was absolutely delighted, saying that I had proved them right – I was successful.

CHAPTER 10

The day that was so important to me had arrived. With my meagre belongings packed, was my dream to be realised? I did hope so.

It was a long train ride to Birmingham, where I was met by car and taken the remaining eighteen miles to the sanatorium. Matron greeted me with a smile. She was tiny and was wearing a navy blue dress with pearl buttons down the front. Her black hair was curled in a braid round her head. We talked for a while, then she asked some questions.

'Have you got a fancy dress? It is New Year's Eve and we are having a party.'

If only she had known, I had worn fancy dresses for a long time: they were almost rags.

'No,' I said, 'I haven't got one,' so she suggested that I could have balloons and go to the party as a balloon lady. Ugh!

I was to share a room with another girl who was also commencing nursing duties. It was an airy room with a large window looking on to the lovely garden. I sat on the bed and wondered what this girl was like. Was she feeling as apprehensive as I was?

It didn't take long to unpack as I didn't have much. There was a knock on the door. 'Nurse, would you come down to the hall?' I nearly looked round, thinking she was talking to someone else.

The big hall was decorated with streamers and balloons. I wished I could have hung mine up also, I felt so silly, clutching five balloons. Music was playing loudly and everyone appeared happy and relaxed. The tables groaned with the weight of so much food; I'd never seen anything like it and wished I could have shared some with my family.

The evening dragged on. I said 'Yes' and 'No', when spoken to but I couldn't relax. When the clock struck twelve midnight we joined hands and sang 'Auld Lang Syne', and another year had begun – 1937.

My room companion was nineteen years old – a delightful girl and very friendly who said she was looking forward to her nursing career. Her parents were not happy with her choice as they considered the work too demanding and too hard; also they were fearful that she would get tuberculosis. Her father was a professional man and she was their only daughter, but she did have two brothers. Her education at a grammar school had stood her in good stead. I didn't say much about my family – there was little for me to brag about – but I told her that I was adamant that I would make my nursing career a successful one.

After a visit to the bathroom, we crawled into bed. It was 1.30 a.m. Two newcomers to the world of medicine with big hearts, big dreams and extremely big heads! The future was full of hope for me but in Europe war clouds were gathering.

I was too excited to sleep, but I knew my companion dozed off. My uniform was on the chair and my little white hat on the dressing table. It was a long night and the call at six o'clock was very welcome. Breakfast was at six thirty. When dressed I looked at myself in the mirror and I liked what I saw. Was this really me? The dress fitted perfectly and I loved the little hat that sat on my head as if it had been there for years.

I enjoyed my breakfast – I hadn't prepared it and didn't have to do the dishes afterwards. I hadn't realised I was so hungry.

The day began. I reported to the ward where I was expected. The hospital had 120 beds. The building was half a wide circle with the outer part made up of glass sliding doors which were open most of the time. The nurses' quarters were above. The patients' beds faced the doors, allowing them to look out on the lovely garden. The terrace of concrete was wide and spacious and, weather permitting, patients were wheeled outside. The foot of each bed was covered with a light rubber overlay which protected them from the weather. Fresh air was definitely a priority for the patients.

On admission, all patients were given a thorough medical examination, then put to bed for a complete rest. Sometimes their stay was as long as three months. As their condition improved, graduated exercises were introduced. It was a slow progress, but their interest had to be maintained as this helped recovery.

Visiting times varied, which was understandable – we were out in the country.

Sometimes concert parties entertained and occasionally the staff put on a concert. I liked these times because I never found it difficult to make a fool of myself, and thought of the acts we had performed at Rabbit Pit Cottage with the gramophone and the one record.

I soon got used to the routine; it wasn't difficult although the hours were long, but I was used to hard work. A sputum mug was on each patient's locker; there was much coughing and these were used for them to spit in. Using handkerchiefs was definitely out. One of my duties was to collect the mugs and take them to a room where they were cleaned and sterilised by one of the porters. This I didn't like doing but it was one of my chores and eventually I was able to do it without thinking.

There were many bed-making sessions and blanket baths. Some of the patients were painfully thin and yet there were others who didn't look ill at all, but all accepted their treatment without complaint, though it must have been very tedious. It was easy to look after them; I loved it, but at the end of the day my bed was a welcome sight.

Diet played a big part in the patients' recovery. The cook was queen of her castle; she produced excellent meals, plain and wholesome, and eventually even I began to fill out. I was used to the open spaces so being in the open air didn't bother me.

No surgery was performed at the hospital. If it was necessary, the patient was transferred to a general hospital.

My salary was small and most of it was sent home. I did think that, with three of us working, conditions at home must have improved but I didn't query it.

Happy? What an understatement that was! Who wouldn't be? The work wasn't hard and I was doing what I had always wanted to do – nursing. We did have an off-duty period during the day, but to go to the shops one would have to catch the bus. Occasionally there was transport available from the hospital. This didn't worry me as I had no money to spend and in any case I had all I needed for the time being.

CHAPTER 11

After two weeks of being on duty I was told to report to the medical superintendent's office; apparently, I was to have a medical examination. All newcomers had to go through this procedure. I hadn't met him but had seen him in the distance. I was apprehensive as I was small for my age and didn't look particularly robust. Supposing I failed this medical examination? What would I do? Where would I go? I was worried – it couldn't bear thinking about.

I knocked on the door and went in. Doctor was sitting at a large desk; he was middle aged with grey hair and of medium build, though he looked very big to me. His eyes were his outstanding feature; they were bright blue, and almost had an hypnotic effect on me.

He asked many questions which I was able to answer quite truthfully, then he told me to strip to the waist and to stand on a certain spot. This I found extremely embarrassing. He didn't speak as he studied me from a distance. Eventually I was allowed to dress and leave his office. I heard afterwards that by viewing the upper part of the body he was able to detect abnormalities in bone structure. As I didn't hear the results of the medical, I assumed that all was well.

I attended lectures on anatomy and physiology and tuberculosis. I didn't find this easy. I was pretty hopeless, but I plodded on – my best friend was my dictionary. Tutor sister was a gem and she did all she could to help and encourage me. Oh, I was envious of those who had had a good education! Sometimes I thought that I could have tried a little harder during my school days.

It was some time before I went home for a break as it was a long way and very costly. Home held no attraction for me. Mother and Dad had moved to Burton-on-Trent, a lovely city. The home situation was so much better and finances much improved.

At the sanatorium the days were full, so much to do, people coming and going all the time. The entertainers and concert groups were very welcome. On one occasion when the staff were entertaining, I was to sing 'Just a Song at Twilight'. My pianist was a ward sister and she gaily played on and left me behind. I tried to catch her up, but I was singing out of tune. She finished first. It wasn't supposed to be funny, but that was how it was received.

One day I borrowed a tennis racquet as the court had a great attraction for me. We did have a few competitions, but it was some time before I was able to compete. The court was officially opened by a well known Whiteman Cup player and at that time I was considered sufficiently competent to be her partner. What an honour! It's a great game and I loved playing.

My spell on night duty gave me time to study as there wasn't much to do; but the odd noises made the darkness very eerie. One morning after dinner – being on night duty this was the end of the night for us – cook said she would bake a chicken and that she would leave it on the table in her sitting room. Tragedy struck during the day when she had a major stroke and died. What a shock for everyone! We were told that she had been prepared for burial by the undertaker and was lying in her room. The chicken – oh, dear, no one was game to go into her room to get it. We wondered what happened to it, but what 'chickens' we were! She was sadly missed.

We were given exams and I managed to scrape through, though I'm sure sister tutor was generous in her marking; maybe she realised how keen I was to succeed.

My twentieth birthday came and went. Birthdays didn't mean much to me, only that I was getting older and should think seriously about general training.

Much later, I discussed this with Matron. She agreed it was time to move on, asking me where I would like to do my general training. I had heard about the London Hospital in the East End of London, which was the largest voluntary hospital at that time in England. It was considered the best. She looked doubtful and said that maybe I was reaching a bit high; then she smiled and said, 'Let's try it,' so I sent for the application form. Looking back I realised how lucky I'd been. I wanted to succeed and with so much help, how could I not go on with this?

When the application form arrived, it was so wonderful that I was able to fill it in myself. That word 'education' again reared its ugly head, but I now had two years of nursing behind me – would it help? I hoped it would. The reply was encouraging and an appointment was made for an interview, to be followed by a medical, should the interview be successful. With fingers crossed on that special day I made my way to the London Hospital. Everyone wished me luck and I realised they were all on my side.

I had told Mother and Dad of my plans and that if I were successful, I would have to sign a contract for four years. Failing to honour this, I would have to pay a few hundred pounds. Dad said, 'Don't worry about that, don't stay if you are unhappy; I'll bail you out, I'll sell the mangle.' What a funny man! I thought of the mangle in the scullery, a metal contraption with two big wooden rollers, which wasn't worth sixpence.

The hospital was situated in the East End of London. After the lovely countryside surrounding the sanatorium, I found the buildings cluttered and grubby. The front of the hospital didn't look very inviting as I entered. It was so big with so much activity, such an atmosphere and above all the smell.

The hall porter directed me to Matron's office where I knocked on the door. Four sisters were seated at their desks looking oh, so professional; my nerve almost failed me as they looked at me, and I thought they were matrons but I realised that they couldn't be. One approached and I said that I had an appointment to see Matron. I was told to take a seat. I watched them as I waited; I asked myself if I really wanted to become one of them. Of course I did!

I was ushered into Matron's office and as we chatted I realised that here was a kind, understanding woman. She did look severe in her uniform, but what was unique about it was the fan shaped cap she was wearing with its two rows of corrugated lace. From the back hung two tails, quite long but not very wide, again with the lace trimmings. I thought it was lovely. She soon put me at my ease.

'Why do you wish to come here to do your general training?' she asked.

The answer was easy, 'Because it is the biggest and the best.'

She spoke very quietly and said I would be accepted providing I passed the medical, which had been arranged. She continued, 'Do you realise you will have to pass the examination set by the General Nursing

Council for England and Wales?' Once again 'education' had reared its ugly head!

I must have looked crestfallen because she said, 'I'm sure you'll have no problem with that.'

The material for the uniform plus a pattern was to be sent to me and she stressed that the pattern must be strictly adhered to. I wondered how I would manage this, and how costly this would be; I had to manage somehow but there would be no financial help from home. After passing the medical I was very pleased that I had been accepted, but there were too many 'ifs' for my liking and my confidence.

Back at the sanatorium Matron was keen to hear what had taken place. I thanked her for providing a reference which must have been excellent. My school teacher once again supplied the second one. She had written that she was following my progress with interest.

The big question remained – how would I prepare for the written educational examination? Apparently it was to take four hours, two in the morning and two in the afternoon: English, maths, history and geography. A few days later the medical superintendent sent for me. He knew about my being accepted at the London Hospital and said he would like to help with the written exam.

He suggested books which might be helpful and said that I could send for them so that they could arrive by post. When this happened I was to go to his office at five o'clock on weekdays and spend half an hour studying written and oral work. I really was in awe of him – his blue eyes seemed to penetrate my very existence – but it was so important that I pass the wretched exam.

Regularly we met for that short time. I did my best but it wasn't good enough for him. He looked at me, rather pathetically, I thought, and said, 'I can't see you passing, you're absolutely hopeless.' I did thank him and deep down I suppose I had to agree with him. I was pleased to get away from those blue eyes. Matron assured me that if I did fail, she would like me to remain at the sanatorium as a staff nurse. This was reassuring as I did so wish to continue nursing.

The day I was to sit for the exam I woke feeling ill and had a high temperature. This was a reaction to the smallpox injection. Matron was concerned and said I really wasn't fit to attend the examination centre in Birmingham, but I insisted that I must attend so she very kindly allowed her driver to take me. The examination room was large, with rows and rows of desks and chairs. I found my seat and with butterflies in my tummy I sat down – it was so quiet and the nervous tension was almost palpable.

The morning flew as I scribbled laboriously, hoping for the best. At lunchtime I was told not to leave the building after the exam as I was to be picked up. I breathed a sigh of relief when it was finished at four o'clock and, not feeling too well, it was lovely to sit in the car to be driven back to the sanatorium.

I went straight to bed and Matron brought me a cup of tea; she was eager to read the exam papers I had brought back with me. No one likes post mortems – she asked many questions and, listening to my answers, she said I shouldn't be too hopeful.

It was a day in March 1939 that I left the sanatorium to report to the training school called Tredegar House in London for six weeks before going on to the hospital. My luggage was heavy; this was filled mostly with my uniform so beautifully made by Matron's dressmaker. I knew full well that if I failed the examination, I would not be allowed to stay at the hospital but that I would be allowed to resit in three months' time – dash the thought.

I was very sad to leave the sanatorium – I'd been there a little over two years. I had matured, weathered the storm as it were, gained confidence and had been given every help possible. I wouldn't mind returning as it was a wonderful hospital but I desperately wanted to do my training. It all depended on that examination.

I had to succeed!

Matron had reminded me of the day I had arrived at the sanatorium. She said I was small and looked so very frail, and she didn't think that I would make the grade. I laughed as I told her how miserable I had felt that New Year's Eve as I had sat in a corner clutching five balloons.

CHAPTER 12

Tredegar House, the training school, was about one mile from the hospital and a very imposing looking building. I rang the doorbell. It was early afternoon, and rather cold. Immediately it was opened by a nursing sister. Another candidate had walked up behind me and I was surprised to hear that her surname was the same as mine. Was it an omen? It had to be, because we were to be friends for the next ten years.

There were many rules and regulations we had to follow, but firstly we lined up to have our uniform checked. The hems had to be eight inches from the ground. Mine was spot on; there were only two who had to let their hems down. What a lot of work! No nonsense here, we had been warned.

Settling down to routine, the days were busy and interesting, there was no time for idle hands. Sometimes lectures were held at the hospital, which was a penny bus ride. The conductors got to know us and teased us – we were a happy lot.

There were certain household chores to be done. It was all part of the training and was shared, but one chore that bugged me was the counting of the china and cutlery. I couldn't understand why this had to be done. Nevertheless, it being my turn one morning, I found a cup and saucer missing. I checked carefully but couldn't find them. Reporting this, I was told in no uncertain terms, 'Check again.' Time was on the wing and I was near to tears; there was a bus to catch as I had to attend a lecture at the hospital. To be late was a disgrace.

I was dismissed, then raced to get the bus. The conductor helped me on, saying, 'Come on, luv, you're running late.' The elusive cup and saucer was found in one of the bedrooms. I had an idea who was responsible, and felt that there should have been an apology.

Our patient, the dummy, was well worn; it had been used and abused for so long by so many hopeful girls. It caused a great deal of amusement

47

many times. Sometimes we had to take its place and we did get rough treatment from inexperienced hands.

There were always some amusing incidents. Thirty-three girls couldn't be serious all the time, and some were real comedians. We played tricks on one another and one day, thinking one of the girls was in the toilet, I tied the two door knobs together. Imagine my horror to hear sister tutor calling out that she was locked in the toilet! I had to confess, but she was a good sort and accepted the incident; in fact, she was very generous.

The maid would call us by ringing a big hand bell at six o'clock; she sounded like the town crier and it was certainly a rude awakening. One evening I tied this bell under the bed of one girl who always retired early. We waited with bated breath for it to ring when she got into bed but it didn't. Lights were turned out at ten o'clock and we were getting worried. As I had put it there, I was the one to retrieve it. She wasn't impressed when I woke her to tell her that she had a bell under her bed. She stared at me through sleepy eyes and said, 'Are you mad? What's the matter with you?' I told her to go back to sleep and I would explain in the morning. I crept back to my room after replacing that wretched bell where it belonged. I believe it took her a while to get back to sleep – I wonder why? We had tried this trick beforehand and it had worked well, but not that night. It did ring when I sat on the bed.

I always enjoyed the practical experience in nursing. My bandaging was good – at least I thought so. I did practise hard but when sister tutor rubbed her hand up and down, the bandage always slipped off.

Doing a spot of detective work I found one other girl had sat the educational exam. She was a tall, awkward looking girl, very quiet and retiring. She said she didn't think she had done well but was hopeful; she desperately wished to make nursing a career, to prove to her parents that she could do it. I asked her if she would do the exam again, which we were allowed to do, but she said, 'No.'

'What about your uniform?' I asked.

She just shrugged her shoulders. She did fail and I didn't see her leave. What a shame – she would have made an excellent nurse!

My results still hadn't arrived; I had forgotten that they were to go to the sanatorium. Eventually a large buff coloured envelope arrived and enclosed was a letter from Matron. She had written, 'Nurse, I have done something I've never done before. I opened your results. Congratulations!

you have passed.'

What a big thrill! I thought of the medical superintendent at the sanatorium and his hypnotic blue eyes. I had proved him wrong. I wasn't hopeless. I was walking on air – the whole future opened for me. I would be a nurse – and a good one! I had a career – me! I'd show them I could amount to anything and my plans were falling into place. Lucky me!!

The time passed all too quickly at Tredegar House. The days were filled with lectures, practical experience and chasing the bus for a penny ride to the hospital.

I always had difficulty in expressing myself and it didn't boost my morale to find written at the bottom of one of my answers. 'What you have written is very interesting, but you haven't answered the question.' Maybe I would get it right one day.

There were times I felt that some of the girls considered themselves superior – that little bit of class distinction kept creeping in. I was envious of those who flaunted their obvious help from their parents, as there was no struggle for them. I didn't let this worry me and told myself I was as good as they, it wasn't my fault that we had struggled to survive. The depression hit us very hard as it did lots of families. Was I better for this? I'm sure I was.

The sixth week we had exams; it was a harrowing time as so much depended on the outcome. The practical exam was a breeze, I'd actually learnt how to put on a bandage without it slipping off. We all passed. What a celebration we had! The dummy was dressed in uniform and abused in the most atrocious way. We did visit interesting places, one being a sewerage farm. I could have thought of a better place to go. It was all part of our education.

CHAPTER 13

What a grand day it was when we became student nurses. My first ward was a Jewish ward where the routine was a little different and so were the meals. They had their own cook. Ward sister was a good disciplinarian but very fair; she expected the best of her nurses at all times. I learnt one word of the Hebrew language: '*nactop*'; I wasn't sure of the spelling, but it meant 'bedpan'.

We reported on duty at seven o'clock after having had breakfast. The patients were made comfortable before being given their breakfast. Sister came on duty at eight o'clock and her first responsibility was to say prayers, the hospital one followed by a regular prayer. Everyone joined in. I liked this very much; it was a lovely way to start the day.

London Hospital Prayer' (Men's Ward)

Almighty and Everloving God, who didst send thine only son Jesus Christ to be the saviour of men, we pray thee as earnestly as we can to bless the work done at the London Hospital. Bless all those rich or poor, who have denied themselves to help the hospital.

This was followed by:

Help all those who are nurses to have always present to their minds the example of our Blessed Saviour's love and sympathy for the poor and suffering. Give them grace and patience faithfully to fulfil their holy calling, doing all as unto thee, and we pray thee to crown their work with success and happiness. We commend, O God, the patients to thy loving care. Soothe their pain; relieve their anxiety; lead them to a knowledge and love of thee; give them patience under their sufferings and a happy ending to all their trouble. We pray thee to remember the wives and children of the men here and help them in their trouble and distress. Grant this we humbly beseech thee, O God, for thy Son Jesus Christ's sake. Amen.

The story goes that one ward sister reading the prayer suddenly stopped as she rubbed her finger along the ledge of her desk, then asked in a loud voice, 'And who was responsible for dusting here?' She continued the prayer. It did cause quite a lot of amusement.

Sister discussed the patients' treatment for the day. Those who were off duty in the morning went away for two hours. The rest went about their duties. Everyone was on duty at meal-times, which was necessary because many patients had to be helped with feeding. At five o'clock the ward was closed, bed-baths given, dressings renewed. After a light supper all activities ceased, curtains were drawn and lights dimmed. It was at this time, providing there were no emergencies and no special treatments, that we were allowed to sit down and study the patients' histories.

As a junior student nurse I spent many hours in the utility room cleaning the bed-pans, etc. – a never ending chore, but it was the same for all of us and we just accepted it. At all times we had to be on our toes as one of the assistant matrons did a ward round daily. I did my best to be missing at those times, but didn't always escape – oh dear, she did ask so many questions. One morning when conducting her round, we were moving slowly from bed to bed and stopped at the foot of one. The patient was wheezing and coughing and she asked for a diagnosis. I couldn't think of the name, so brightly said, 'She has a chest complaint.' Sister didn't say anything but as she left the ward she asked for my name. I was very worried – that's done it, I thought, I'll be told to go for sure. Hastily I checked the patient's chart to read that she had 'bronchial asthma'. I certainly remembered that for ever.

We were each given a black and a white book. In the black book we had to record the ward and the amount of time spent there. This was a true record as we travelled through the hospital. The white book was a bit more complicated. It contained a list of practical work that had to be carried out, seen and signed by either ward sister or staff nurse. This wasn't easy, firstly to have time to do the tasks and secondly to get them

51

checked so that they could be ticked off. A certain number of these items had to be completed each month and the full list finished before the hospital finals, which were taken after three years' training.

Our salary for the first year was eighteen pounds; this increased for second and third year. For me this money had to stretch a long way. Shoes, black; stockings, black; toiletries, etc. all had to be bought. Books were expensive, but there was always a little to send home.

Six months at the hospital and things were going really well, but there were many rumours that war was imminent. Questions were asked. Would Hitler agree to Chamberlain's request? Chamberlain thought so, he was sure his last meeting had been successful. There'd be no war.

Unfortunately it wasn't to be and the grim declaration was made over the wireless. We were at war with Germany. It was 3 September 1939.

There was excitement in the air, and a lot of optimism. The war won't last long, let's get it over with, but there were those who were pessimistic, saying, 'We'll all be killed.' As for me, I was cross, maybe a little selfish; I was on my way to being a qualified nursing sister; what now, I asked myself? There wasn't time to dream. I was told to pack, as with others I was being evacuated. Things moved very quickly and after packing I joined the other nurses to board the bus. Apparently we were being sent to a hospital outside London. As juniors we wouldn't be much help in caring for the acute cases which were expected.

London was expected to be one of the first cities to be bombed because it was the capital and because of the docks and being the main shipping centre. The king and queen resided there, and there were many historical buildings. Two thirds of the hospital was to be evacuated and only a trained skeleton staff stayed behind. Some children were evacuated and I thought what a heartbreak for their parents to let them go, but the East End of London was definitely a target for bombers.

The bus was crowded with chattering females, all wanting to know answers and yet knowing there were none forthcoming, at least not yet. We arrived at a town in Essex called Billericay, after a journey of about 1½ hours, a very pleasant ride through the countryside. England was a lovely place; there was no wonder that Hitler wanted to add it to his conquests.

We arrived at the hospital, which was small and had only a tiny medical unit as it housed mainly the elderly. As we alighted from the bus in the driveway, the siren sounded, the first one: an ear-splitting noise which sent a chill through the body, and we all dropped to the ground. Shocked, Matron called out, 'Spread out, nurses, I don't want you all killed at once.' The all-clear followed immediately; it had been a false alarm. Getting up, we looked very foolish as we brushed ourselves; fortunately, it wasn't wet but we did look a grubby lot. It was then that Matron realised what she had called out, and we saw the funny side of it. What a laugh we had!

There was no accommodation for us at the hospital so we were to be billeted out. Oh! lucky me, I was to stay with Mrs Wood and her daughter Marjorie. Theirs was a lovely home only a short distance away. They had two cocker spaniels which I thought were an added bonus. Nicky was the name of the younger one and Podge, a golden colour, who was as fat as his name suggested.

The garden was lovely, spacious, with trees, flowers and shrubs. I gazed in awe around me. Could I be back at the 'big house' with all its luxuries? How my life had changed! It didn't take me long to settle in and I was to spend many months there off and on all through my training and until I left England to go to Australia. I realised that it wasn't easy for Mrs Wood and Marjorie to take in a boarder, as Mrs Wood was in her early seventies and was totally deaf; and for Marjorie in her early thirties it was more responsibility. She was her mother's ears and how patient she was! The government allowed them one guinea a week to look after us. They did have a full time domestic, but this luxury soon came to an end as she had to leave to drive a milk cart.

Big changes took place at the hospital and Nissen huts shot up like mushrooms, housing thirty beds. These were in rows with enough room for a locker between them, just like sardines in a tin. The huts were heated with pot belly stoves and fed with coke, and if they went out they were brutes to relight.

Most of the elderly were either sent home or to other institutions. The ones remaining had to be taught air-raid drill. They had to take their pillows and get under a bed and we were expected to lie with them. It was a very sad situation for some, as they were confused and thought they had to take off their clothes. It was on one of these occasions that my male patient, having already crawled under the bed, wished to go to the toilet, but before I could help he spied an open window and aimed through it!

The huts filled quickly with all types of patients, both medical and surgical cases. The operating theatre was very small with the windows bricked and blackened. On one occasion when major surgery was in progress the lights failed, including the emergency ones. Candles and torches proved unsatisfactory and panic was beginning to set in when someone had a brainwave – why not use the sun? The sterilising room wasn't blackened and bricked so with the use of two large stainless steel trays, the sun was reflected onto the site of the operation. It was successful and the operation was completed. The patient made a good recovery and wasn't told of the drama that had taken place. Although the end result was a success, it was an emergency that we could have done without. In the darkness, the tense situation was felt by all, especially the surgeon. There was an unconscious patient on the table with his abdomen open, and he was responsible. He had been able to ligate the oozing blood vessels with the aid of a torch. Because of the war, emergencies were frequent.

The bombing continued in earnest and we got used to the sound of the German planes; they were always heading for London and we were in their flight path – not a comforting thought because they could off-load their bombs if they had failed to drop them on the target. This occasionally happened, causing much damage. Sometimes we watched the Spitfires, those daring single-seated fighter planes, weaving in and around the formation of the bombers, causing havoc. Some were able to get direct hits.

I met a number of these pilots and what a dedicated bunch! Dressed in their uniform they looked oh, so gorgeous; they certainly made my heart flutter. I wondered about their families and, most of all, their futures. Would they survive this awful war? This uncertainty was, I suppose, for all of us.

My hostess would want to go outside first to see what was happening. She was a very determined little lady, and being totally deaf didn't help. Marjorie was involved in driving a van containing food and drinks to the bombed areas. We tried to arrange our duties so that there was always someone home with her. We had an arrangement that if I heard activity overhead and maybe bombs falling while we were in the lounge during the evening, I was to tap her on her knee and we would then get under the old oak table. I'm not sure that this would have protected us from falling debris but we were hopeful.

Well, one evening it happened as we had planned. Mrs Wood was sorting buttons on her lap when I heard the drone of the planes overhead and then there was a loud swishing noise. I didn't tap her on her knee – I gave her an almighty bang. She shot up in the air with buttons going in all directions, and we headed for the old oak table but we couldn't get underneath as we were so convulsed with laughter. Surprisingly, nothing happened and I thought that I must have been hearing things. She wasn't impressed but her agility had amazed me. While picking up the buttons, there was a bang on the front door and a voice called out, 'We need help out here.' It was the voice of the warden. Going outside, what a sight! Everywhere was lit up just like a fairy land. It had been a Molotov basket full of incendiary bombs that had fallen and exploded on reaching the ground. Apparently they were used to light up the targets for the following bombers. We had buckets of water and sand handy, as all householders had to be thus prepared, so it was all hands on deck. There was an oil bomb on the garage and one on the roof but fortunately they didn't burn long. Then it was back to the lounge to pick up the remaining buttons. We had been very lucky; maybe it wasn't our turn yet?

I loved these two dear people; they were very good to me and I was very happy in their lovely home. I was to keep in touch for years, and I would never have met them if war had not broken out. My memories of Mrs Wood, my hostess, are always tinged with the smell of lavender. Each year she collected it around the neighbourhood. She would lay it on a sheet to dry, then shred it, put the seeds in a pillowcase and send it to a children's hospital. The house was saturated with the lovely lavender smell. In spite of her age and deafness, she was a wonderful woman who was always ready to give a helping hand. During my stay there she was very interested in my welfare and encouraged me to study, read *The Times* and listen to the news. 'You can never learn too much,' was her motto. I know my education improved a lot while there.

Marjorie taught country dancing on the lawn at the local manor when she had time; she told me I danced like an elephant. What a compliment, but also what fun!

To study under wartime conditions was extremely difficult, but it had

55

to be done as there was a deadline to meet. We slept on single mattresses on the lounge floor. I remember that the night before the preliminary exam there was much activity overhead and bombs fell in the distance. As I closed my eyes to sleep I was convinced that I wouldn't be there in the morning, so I didn't worry about the exam. I slept soundly. I sat the exam and somehow passed with flying colours. My twelve months there had been no drawback.

CHAPTER 14

I kept in touch with home but was shattered when a telegram arrived from Mother saying that Dad had died. How could this be? I was beside myself wondering what had happened. Owing to transport difficulties the telegram had been delayed. I was given compassionate leave immediately and after throwing a few things in a case, Marjorie drove me to catch a train for Burton-on-Trent.

In London I changed trains. The station was a hive of activity; men and women in uniform were everywhere. I was in full uniform as I hadn't bothered to change, and I remember very clearly sitting in the corner of the carriage, distraught and very unhappy. The carriage was full and I was surprised when a young man came along and asked me for my identity card. 'Certainly,' I said, 'But first may I see yours?' He obliged and smiled. Mine was in my case and while fumbling for it, the contents fell out on the floor. Very calmly he helped me pick them up and put them back, handing me a pair of knickers – a display I could have done without. This caused some amusement to the other passengers and even I had to smile. He was a transport detective and had been curious about my uniform. It did attract a lot of attention outside London.

Arriving home I just screamed at Mother. Why? why? I needed answers. She said Dad had been in hospital for a week. He had had major surgery for a bowel obstruction. She had visited him during the afternoon and left him quite well; he must have had an embolism, a blood clot, because he was dead one hour later. She said she was surprised as he appeared to be making a good recovery, and she didn't want to worry me, so hadn't let me know. I was very upset as I had so wanted to tell him that I had passed the preliminary exam. The funeral was a small affair and as the coffin was lowered into the grave, I thought what a rotten married life Dad had had. Just as things had turned the corner, with finances improved and a decent home, he had to get sick. I asked myself, 'Was this fair?' Nevertheless, there wasn't anything to keep me home so I returned to the hospital, where I got a wonderful welcome.

The experience at the hospital was good considering the extreme conditions, but the will to survive was uppermost in our minds. Some of the Nissen huts filled very quickly with soldiers, and most were enjoying the rest. Who could blame them?

Early one morning I woke with abdominal pain and was diagnosed as having acute appendicitis, so, instead of being the theatre nurse, I was the patient. The operation was straightforward and I was sent home to convalesce for two weeks.

One day while I was there, Mother asked if I would like to go to a spiritualist meeting; she said she didn't go regularly but that she found it interesting. I wasn't a believer in that sort of thing but was curious so I went with her. The hall was large and many people were already there. The medium sat at a small table on the stage. We sang a hymn and sat down. She said a few words of welcome, then pointed in my direction. I looked round, thinking it was to someone behind but she said, 'Yes, you.

'Standing behind you I see an elderly gentleman. He has very little hair and has a grey beard. His arm is in a sling, and he is very interested in what you are doing and if you need help, you only have to ask. I see you in a large building and whatever you are doing you will be successful.'

All very weird and interesting. She had described my grandfather and when he died his arm was in a sling. I was in a big building and hoping to complete my nursing career.

She continued talking to others, then the meeting was closed. I shook hands with her on the way out and she asked what I was doing. I told her.

'Do you believe in lucky charms?'

'No,' I said.

'Well, think about it and get a small pig and put it on a piece of mauve ribbon.'

This was rather intriguing because Mother's mother, as well as being a midwife, also kept pigs at the bottom of her garden. The night before I was born one of her pigs had been killed for food. This made an impression on me and a few years later, seeing a lucky charm pig in a shop, I bought it and popped it in my handbag. On telling that story to a friend she gave me a piece of mauve ribbon.

I was pleased to get back to hospital although Mother had done her best to make me comfortable. There were no interruptions on the train this time but there was the feeling that everyone was rushing to complete jobs.

On the whole everyone played their part and when a request from the War Office for aluminium was announced, everyone gladly gave their saucepans. It was amazing how we all adapted to war-time conditions. Incendiary bombs became a regular nightly occurrence, a nuisance and a danger. My friend Muriel, with her usual humour, remarked that she was awakened by a swishing noise and found she had a dear little oil bomb burning by the side of her bed. It had burned through the roof. It was disposed of very quickly.

Some of the hospital beds were occupied by German patients who were treated well, like our own pilots – they were just carrying out their orders. One morning while stripping a bed I found a note under the pillow. In broken English it read, 'Thank you for looking after me.' Those men were transferred to camp hospitals when able to travel.

As we watched the 'dog fights', and that was often, we saw one Spitfire pilot bale out while his plane swooped to the ground in a ball of fire. We were appalled to see a German plane shooting at him as he came down in his parachute.

My time was up at that hospital; I had been there eighteen months, and the hospital had spread beyond recognition. It was now a very busy medical and surgical hospital and the patients were given the best treatment. I was very sad to leave. I had matured, become more responsible, and was on my way to reaching my goal, to be a registered nursing sister.

For me it was back to the London Hospital.

CHAPTER 15

It was a dull day when I arrived at the underground. It was very busy and I could see people carrying some of their belongings on their backs. Whitechapel was a sad sight, unrecognisable with many of the buildings just heaps of rubble. To me it was a tragedy.

There was the usual flow of traffic but at a much slower pace. People were making their way with a grim, determined look on their faces but one could see that they would accept whatever Hitler threw at them – they wouldn't give in. No matter what, they would make the best of a bad situation.

The underground stations were a haven for some families. Every evening they would line up to claim their spot on the platform, clutching their meagre belongings, some dragging their reluctant children. Even animals were brought with them. How they were able to sleep I don't know. There was always someone around who had a musical instrument, and to get off the train to the sounds of 'Roll out the Barrel', and 'I'm going to hang out the washing on the Siegfried Line', certainly boosted one's morale. Somehow there was always a feeling of optimism and their sense of humour never wavered. There was a funny side to everything or they made it look that way; they were full of hope, survival uppermost in their mind and 'togetherness' shone through.

Air-raid shelters had shot up like mushrooms; some were well stocked with food, stretchers, etc. One air-raid warden was very worried during a raid as he watched the people hastily going inside his fairly large shelter. Being a conscientious fellow, he called out, 'Anyone here pregnant?' From the back a Cockney voice answered, ''Ave a 'eart, mate, we ain't had time yet.' Such was their humour and their acceptance of the traumas associated with war.

Many people had a small primitive air-raid shelter at the bottom of their garden, a very deep hole lined and covered with corrugated iron. I never had an occasion to use one of these but they served a purpose.

Posters were displayed everywhere carrying messages such as, 'Be like Dad, keep mum', 'Careless talk costs lives'. There were many and they couldn't be missed.

On the domestic front there were suggestions as to how to save water, food, and fuel for heating. I remember reconstituting dried egg powder and was surprised at its flavour. There was powdered milk, orange juice and cod liver oil for small children and pregnant mothers. I believe that during the war we were much healthier.

I very soon settled down in the hospital, which was a hive of activity. Acute, accident and war casualties were admitted. The patients were transferred to hospitals outside London when they were well enough. All mattresses had ropes tied to the ends and should an emergency arise, the mattress with the patient on it would be placed on the floor and dragged to a safer part of the hospital. I don't know if this exercise was put to use, certainly not while I was there.

The upper wards had been closed, but the many rooms in the basement were put to good use. No need to say that the operating theatres were in constant use, and there were times when the entrance hall was crowded with patients on stretchers waiting for attention.

Was I nervous during a bombing raid? Only when I was off duty. On duty I had no time for nerves. The hospital was hit a number of times and part of the laundry was put out of action, which did create a real problem. With the restriction of the water supply we became adept at washing in very little.

A delayed action bomb landed on the tennis court which was in the courtyard surrounded by some of the hospital wards. The bomb squad was quickly on the scene and told us it weighed approximately 650 lbs. They did take enormous chances and, listening to the tick, they could predict the time it would explode. They should have been named, 'The Suicide Squad'. A wall of sandbags was placed round it and when it did explode, the sandbags hung on the power lines like dirty washing.

Our training continued with lectures in our off duty time, and tests occurred regularly. If on night duty, we were expected to get up and do them. Our weekly rations included 2 ozs butter and 4 ozs sugar. Sometimes I had a little butter left over, but not sugar because I had a sweet tooth. When I was home on one occasion Mother took my ration book to the butcher's but he could only give her a small tin of corned beef which was my week's ration. We were issued with gas masks and some of us with steel helmets which were to be carried at all times.

Night duty had its many draw-backs because it wasn't easy sharing with others in a confined space and with the noise of the intermittent bombing. There were no set hours for the medical staff; they were on call twenty-four hours, which was very tiring for them. The administrative staff did a wonderful job, as the hospital was well organised and the nursing staff swapped around. I know we were happy to get out of London for a spell. The siren sounded regularly; it became monotonous and people tended to ignore it. The East End was in ruins; what further damage could be done?

My turn for a transfer came round yet again and this time it was to Brentwood, not far from Billericay where I had spent many months. How lovely! It was only a short bus ride to visit my dear friends. I felt like yelling, 'See you soon.'

The hospital there comprised large huts, two of which were in use for the nursing staff. It was well established and well run. Occasionally we were interrupted with sirens and the bombing, but it was not as noisy as in London. Routine was the same with the lectures and tests cropping up regularly, and I was still struggling to express myself on paper. The sister tutor must have been frustrated as she ploughed through my answers. I joined the student nurses' association which organised different activities. It was amazing what could be made with scraps of material and we had an exhibition, charging one penny for admission. Muriel was a wonderful knitter and we had a baby corner, with the proceeds going to a charity. I acquired an old parachute and, like many others, spent hours unpicking seams – a slow, tedious job. I made myself a pair of knickers and a petticoat; they looked all right but were uncomfortable to wear. We had been issued with clothing coupons which didn't allow us to keep up with the fashion, so we were very pleased to get any 'free-bees'.

One evening we had a spelling competition and I entered, paying a penny. What hope did I have? Surprising myself and the other competitors, I won it. My prize was a small jar of sugar, I don't know who donated it, but to me it was a jar of gold.

We were full of ideas and decided to produce a magazine. I offered to write an article and call it 'Cubicle Chatter'. As the hut was divided into cubicles by curtains, I thought that would be easy. One evening, sitting on my bed with pad and pen, I jotted down what I heard. It was interesting – some were to have a medical the following day and their conversation was intriguing; they were undecided as to what colour underwear they would wear. I thought that very amusing as I scribbled away. The magazine was published with only one issue, I wonder why!

I invited Mother to come for a short stay while I was there as it was easy to find accommodation for her. We did travel to London to see a show in the West End, but London held no attractions for me. She was surprised to see so much devastation and was only too pleased that she didn't live there. We talked quite a lot, but although we understood one another better, there was no way she was going to answer my questions about the 'big house'.

I couldn't understand this and told her so, but her answer was crisp and to the point. 'We'll let sleeping dogs lie.' She'd enjoyed her short break, but I felt she was pleased to be going back to a routine she had made for herself over the years.

CHAPTER 16

During my stay at Brentwood, I met Richard. He was a tall, good looking fellow, a Sergeant in the Army. I'm not sure what happened, but I was immediately attracted to him. It must have been the same for him.

He had been visiting one of his mates in the ward I was on duty in, and accidentally bumped into me. Apologising, he asked, 'Are you all right?' He introduced himself and asked if we could meet some time. Hastily I told him that I would be off duty at four o'clock the following afternoon and would meet him outside the hospital. I could see that he wanted to talk; I did too, but I was busy and to stand around talking to soldiers was frowned upon, so I said, 'See you tomorrow.'

I thought about him a lot as I carried out my nursing duties. I'd never been involved with a young man before and the thought was exciting. It was the beginning of a wonderful friendship which blossomed into love. He told me that he lived in Wales and that he was stationed near the hospital with his unit. His next move would be overseas.

We became very close, Richard was very loving and I responded to his caresses; this hadn't happened to me before and it was a great feeling. Sexually the desire was there and we talked about it many times, but I thought it would be stupid to go all the way as life was so uncertain. I knew it was hard for him but he assured me that I could trust him. We did get close to our natural desires which was not easy to control, but sanity prevailed. I admired him and loved him so much.

Then suddenly he wasn't there – he had gone overseas and it was truly heartbreaking. We had been meeting when we could for six months. I had learnt what love was, to be kissed, hugged and cuddled and to be needed.

Now he was gone!!

We corresponded. He wrote beautiful letters, but couldn't say where he was, as all letters were censored. We talked about the future and made big plans. He said he would like to start an antique business when the war was over. I smiled at this and pictured myself cleaning old furniture – a dirty job. But there was no future for Richard and me! He was killed in action at Dunkirk. I heard this afterwards. Like so many others, in that wretched war I had loved and lost.

The hospital final was drawing near and I was very apprehensive as exams really did bother me. I was approaching my twenty-fourth birthday and time was moving forward so fast. This exam was very important because failure meant leaving the hospital. That was a severe rule, I thought.

My friend Muriel was a great help and we always studied together. Before the exam we spent a few days in Coventry with her parents. They were delightful people and I was amazed at the lovely meals her mother produced for us. I think she must have saved their food coupons to use especially for us. Muriel was a pianist and during the evening we had some lovely sing-songs round the piano.

Coventry had taken a real beating and while we were there the Cathedral received a direct hit. The one that has replaced it, although attractive, doesn't have that old world charm.

Once again for me it was back to London. My stay in Brentwood had gone quickly and it seemed that we were always on the move. The powers-that-be knew what they were doing, I suppose, and it certainly didn't harm us. In fact I think we were better for it. There was very little time to dwell on the miseries surrounding us. Life went on and most East Enders lived in their basements, the underground, and the shelters.

The day for the examination arrived and there were many butterflies in my tummy, but I wasn't the only one with this problem. The practical side never worried me, I always got a credit pass, but the theory – ugh! I don't remember much about the questions but it was a great relief to see my name on the pass list. The state final followed soon after and I knew I hadn't done well. In fact, I was the only one who failed out of a class of thirty-one.

This was considered a disgrace and I had to make an appointment to explain to Matron why this had happened. I was made to wait two weeks and it was agony as I pondered my future. Would I be allowed to sit again? Eventually I was ushered into her office. Her first question was, 'Why have you failed?' I was very nervous as I stuttered an answer and mumbled about how I had botched up the medical paper. We talked about this; she was very understanding and very fair and her knowledge of me, just small fry in a busy hospital, surprised me. She smiled and said that I would be allowed to resit in three month's time – in the meantime I would be sent to a medical hospital to gain medical experience. Then she wished me good luck. I left her office with a sigh of relief, and vowed I would never forget her.

It was two weeks before that move which was to be for my own benefit, to spend time in a medical ward. This hospital in Enfield was a converted school but still a branch of the London Hospital. It would help, I supposed, but deep down I knew that my problem was the difficulty of expressing myself on paper.

The building was large and imposing with only the ground and first floor in use. I was to report to the sister-in-charge, on the first floor. Approaching the stairs, I was halted by a voice coming from the top. I looked up. A sister was standing there, arms folded, staring down at me.

She said, 'Are you my new staff nurse?' When I answered, 'Yes', she continued, 'I've a very busy ward of fifty-two patients and what use will you be to me, nurse? You failed the state final exam which means you cannot give drugs without their first being checked, not even an aspirin, nurse.' Unhappily I thought that this episode of my life didn't look as if it would be easy, and I mounted the stairs to join her.

Once again I was billeted out, a walk of about thirty minutes. The house was large and the entrance hall was spacious, with many beautiful pictures on the wall. In fact, there were pictures everywhere – it was like a museum.

I was shown to a bedroom cluttered with antique furniture, and in the middle was a very large iron bed. I thought that I would get lost in that, but apparently I was to share it with another nurse. I decided that it was going to be very interesting sharing a bed with a complete stranger. It was amazing what happened in war-time and had to be accepted.

I met my bed-mate later in the evening and she was a delightful person, bubbling with personality and extremely funny. She had passed her state final and was sympathetic when she heard my tale of woe. We were to snuggle together in that big bed – bother the war, bother everything, at least we had a bed. Rumour had it that a murder had been committed in that very room but we didn't care. The wardrobes were so big that anyone could hide there; we couldn't fill them.

My room-mate put on some very good acts about this, causing much laughter. There was a ghost, she said, that wandered around in the dead of night. 'I've seen it,' she said with a twinkle in her eye. How could I believe her? Her imagination ran riot. It didn't worry me whether the room was haunted or not or if the murderer's ghost did wander around at night; there were murders being committed daily because of the war. I asked myself, when would it all end?

I reported on duty at seven o'clock not feeling confident or optimistic, but resolved that I would do my best. As sister had said, there were fifty-two patients including eight children. All were medical cases needing tender loving care. As a hospital that 'school', in my opinion, wasn't very practical but needs must. The corridor was long with the small rooms leading off. By the end of the day I'm sure we clocked up quite a number of miles. I found it extremely difficult to care for the patients, to watch them as was necessary for their welfare in this situation.

One morning the big white chief, the physician, followed by his entourage of medical students, was doing his round in the children's ward. One of the children, a boy aged seven, was drawing on the wall with a crayon. I took the crayon from him. Immediately the big white chief turned to me, saying. 'Nurse, would you take a bone from a dog?'

'No, sir, of course not.'

'Then give the boy back his crayon,' he said with a grin.

'Can't do that, sir,' I replied, 'Matron would not be too impressed with the mess.'

I gave the boy a pencil and paper and asked him to draw on that. We moved on. I knew he was a family man and wondered if his walls at home were covered with crayon – I believe they could have been.

Stopping at the foot of the bed of a lovely little five-year-old he read his medicine list. Turning to the medical student in charge, he asked if he had ordered the special drug written there. 'Yes,' he said. Turning to me he asked if the child had been given that amount and when I said 'No,' he asked why not.

'The dose was too high.'

'Then how much did you give?'

'One eighth,' I replied.

Nothing more was said until we left the ward. He told the medical student to take more care and that he should be grateful I hadn't given the dose he had ordered, as it could have had disastrous results. I talked to the student afterwards, said I was sorry that it had happened, but reminded him that when he wrote it down I had said that it was much too high. He was a keen young man and I thought he would make a good doctor.

Our hours were long and we got tired. There was no set time for war, it happened, the damage was done. I trudged home one evening about half-past ten. It was dark and planes could be heard heading for London as usual. I sighed, 'Poor old London.'

Mulling over my thoughts of the day's activity, the silence was suddenly shattered as the guns blazed away from a nearby field. Searchlights streamed across the sky searching for the planes. The noise was deafening. I covered my ears and jumping into a hedge I yelled, 'Stop it! Stop it!' It was a few seconds before I realised what I was doing and I did feel foolish as I brushed the twigs and leaves off my uniform. Feeling relieved that no one had heard me, I continued on my way. The searchlights were very powerful and would occasionally focus on a plane, I was too tired to care, my big bed beckoned.

Sister reported sick after I had been there for three weeks; she did look so tired. I was sad to see her go; she was a good nurse. It hadn't taken me long to find out that her bark was worse than her bite. For the time being there was no one to replace her so I had to carry on.

In a hospital ward funny incidents do happen from time to time. When one woman patient was admitted, I noticed she was wearing a wig, so I sent nurse to comb her hair. She didn't recognise the wig and when she put the comb through, the wig came off. She gave a yell and dropped the comb. Everyone enjoyed the joke, including the patient.

On admission all patients had their hair inspected. I find this isn't done these days; I wonder why.

There was another incident concerning this patient. During the early hours of one morning after a bad dream she got out of bed and was crawling on her hands and knees along the corridor. She had lost her wig and the light was shining on her bald shiny scalp. Nurse had been busy in the kitchen and was carrying a tray of mugs, when she rounded the corner of the corridor and saw that apparition crawling towards her. She yelled and dropped the tray and I got a fright too – I had been busy attending to a baby. Hastily we put the poor dear to bed; she was rather confused, but she did make a full recovery. I never did find out why she had lost her hair.

Night duty was eerie as only the minimum shaded lights were allowed. I was supposed to be studying for the state final. What a hope!! There was no time on duty and I was too tired off duty.

The hike to and from the hospital was time consuming, while the intermittent gun-fire didn't help the nerves. For me there were no set hours nor had other trained staff. We went home when we finished.

Another night while writing the report the silence was shattered as a woman patient called out in a loud voice, 'George, take your bloody cold feet off me.' I smiled and thought that at least she had George in bed with her.

There were many stories to tell but not all had a happy ending. We did our best under some very difficult situations. On a lighter note, I often wondered why men make such a noise when passing wind. In the quiet of the night, combined with their snoring, it could become quite musical. I remember reading an epitaph on a grave which went like this:

'Where'er you are, where'er you be, always let your wind go free, for it was the wind that killeth me.'

We all do it, but maybe women are a little more refined.

It was frustrating not being able to check drugs and the trained staff on the ground floor were not impressed because they had to do it for me and they were so busy.

At last came the state final exam – I hadn't studied, I had had no time and was too tired anyway. Just to open a book was a sedative, and I fell asleep. 'Pen, do your work,' I told myself. The practical experience had been excellent, all I had to do was to write about it.

I passed! Having now completed my staff year, I reported back to the London Hospital as a State Registered Nurse. This was a wonderful feeling; it had taken a long time and what a long way I had travelled!

As usual London was a depressing sight and I hated it. The V2 rockets shattered a city that was already in ruins, then there was a new menace called 'doodle bugs'. What next? These were small unmanned planes that roared across the sky, the tail of which appeared to be on fire. They were programmed where to go and on reaching their destination, they just dropped out of the sky. The bombs and rockets were dreadful, but the doodle bugs were devastating – they were so frightening and caused so much misery and uncertainty.

I remember on one occasion when I was visiting my friends in Billericay, seeing one of the doodle bugs roar past the window. It was very low and I realised that it would drop out of the sky any moment. I lay down on the floor and put my hands over my ears. It dropped in the wood nearby and what an explosion. The house shook but how grateful I was that it had dropped in the wood, and not on the houses nearby.

I was very sad to leave my comedian bed-partner; she had been a real tonic and I had enjoyed her company so much. But at last I was to catch up with my namesake who, like me, had been travelling round the different branches of the London Hospital. Having passed her state final first time, she had also completed her staff year.

The question arose – what now? We both wished to do midwifery, so once again we discussed this with Matron – I remember at the time, did I see a twinkle in her eye? I believe so. She said she would be pleased for us to stay at the hospital to do the training in the midwifery section, but we wanted to get away from London as it was so depressing. We thanked Matron; it was an honour to be asked but we had discussed the possibility of becoming Queen's Nurses at a centre in Birmingham. She wished us every success and hoped that she would hear from us from time to time. This we agreed to do. I admired her so much; all through my general training she had been there to encourage me – what more could a person wish for?

We were accepted to train as Queen's Nurses.

I had corresponded with Matron at the Sanatorium and she invited me to visit. I stayed with her for a week. It was most enjoyable and when I told her of my plans to do midwifery, she presented me with a book – *A Handbook of Midwifery* by Comeyns, Berkerley. I also said 'Hello' to the medical superintendent; his blue eyes twinkled but all he said was, 'You surprised us all.'

CHAPTER 17

The trip to Birmingham was uneventful and we presented ourselves to the nurses' home.

With a population of over one million, Birmingham was Britain's second largest city. Mentioned in the Doomsday book, it developed slowly until the middle of the sixteenth century when it had already established its reputation as a small industrial town.

In a comfortable nurses' home there was Matron and the supervisor and six trained nurses whose job it was to care for the sick in their homes. The area was divided and Muriel, who had had very little experience riding a bike, was given the city. I offered to swap. I had been riding a bike all my life, so it seemed. She said she would manage. I had very little traffic to cope with and admired Muriel for sticking to her guns, but I was a little worried, as in the city there were tram lines.

Our duties varied and the diabetics claimed our first attention as their injections were to be given before breakfast. Some were able to inject themselves. I would have hated to do this myself, and admired the patients who did.

Then there was the general care, and some were long-standing bed cases, mothers needing help with young babies, and any nursing duty we were called upon to do.

Some cases were very distressing. A young man in his early thirties, confined to bed, had cancer in the groin. On my first visit his sister met me at the door, a look of concern on her face.

'Oh dear,' she said, 'You're not the district nurse, you are so young; we were expecting someone much older.' I soon put her at her ease and followed her up the stairs to meet her brother. He was reading a book and I was surprised how well he looked.

'Hello, nurse.' He said his name was Charles. I sat on his bed and we talked for a while. He was well educated and had been a school principal before he had taken ill. He confided in me that the love of his life was music; it was mine also, though I had had very little time to indulge.

With his dressing completed, he had overcome his embarrassment and we found we had a lot in common.

I visited him daily and we became firm friends. What would have happened if he hadn't been dying of cancer? I don't suppose I would have met him. One day he said that he had planned to write a book and that he would dedicate it to me. It would have been an honour but I knew that it wouldn't materialise. He had attended hospital and had had specialised treatment which hadn't helped. His doctor had told me that because of secondaries in his liver, it was only a matter of time. His family was wonderful. His dear old dad in his early eighties was so distressed and his sister always had a cup of tea and a scone waiting for me when I had finished his dressing.

Charles confided that he had been a church organist and asked if I had noticed his grand piano in the lounge. Of course I had – a magnificent instrument.

'Oh, to be able to play it or even hear it played,' he said. As Muriel was a pianist I asked her if she would play for him. This was no problem for her, so it was decided we would spend our next half day off with him. This we had once a fortnight. Charles was excited as he sorted through his music, and Muriel brought some too. We opened all the doors and it was a real musical evening. Sadly, Charles' condition deteriorated after a severe haemorrhage and he died soon after. I was very sad as we had been so close.

Sometimes life can be very cruel. We had been warned in our early training not to get emotionally involved with our patients, but I did with Charles and I brushed away a silent tear as I cycled to my next case.

The London Hospital uniform wasn't suitable for riding a bike, but I was very proud of it and had no intention of changing it. One day when crossing an intersection that was controlled by a policeman, he stared as I cycled past and called out, 'My God, nurse, where did you get that hat?' To me that hat was a symbol; it perched on my head like a chamber pot upside down. It had a large velvet bow on the front and was fastened with ribbon under the chin. The coat had cape sleeves and was eight inches from the ground. Many people stared at me as I cycled round the district.

During the morning I was supposed to have a drink. I sometimes had a cup of tea and a bun, and for this we were allowed sixpence. This didn't happen very often because the patients were always generous and we were offered many cups of tea, in all sorts of receptacle from mugs, broken, chipped, cracked, with no handles, to the very special china.

There was a small café in my district which was popular with the locals. One morning there were two men having a cup of tea and a cigarette. They stared at me as I sat down at the table near them, and I couldn't help but hear one say, 'What do you reckon she does?'

'Well,' said the other, 'She doesn't belong to the Salvation Army, they don't wear a hat like that.'

'Perhaps she's one of those people who pray for the sick before they die.'

They continued chatting, watching me; I didn't enlighten them but I was highly amused.

Some of my patients were pathetic individuals and one little lady was no exception. She would spend the day alone leaning on the fire guard, throwing small lumps of coal on the fire to keep warm. The coal didn't always land in the fire, and when I arrived she would be black with her face stained from blackened hands, but she always had a smile for me. She never said very much; there were many questions I wanted to ask her but she was reluctant to talk about her situation. Her husband would get her up in the morning and after giving her her breakfast would sit her in this position before going to work. He would have to carry her as she was paralysed from the waist down. What his job was I never found out, but she said he would pop home at around midday to put her on the commode. There was a sixteen-year-old daughter, but I didn't meet her. She wasn't any help to her parents but who could really blame her? The situation was very difficult and I did my best for her. I would sponge her all over and then see that she had something to eat. Once a week I would give her an enema, and that day she would be left in her bed. There was so much this patient needed, but I was very busy and could only share some of my time with her. Would she have been happier in hospital? That question wasn't asked.

We were very busy and new cases were always coming in. One of these was a woman in her late sixties who was blind and wore glass eyes, which had to be removed daily and the sockets washed. She lived just round the corner from the nurse's home, so wasn't on anyone's district. Not surprisingly no one wanted this job, so we tossed for it. I was the winner.

Not feeling very confident, I knocked on her door and walking in, wished her a 'good morning'. She was sitting in her kitchen, a buxom woman, and as she turned her head in the direction of my voice, those glass eyes, a bright blue, looked almost normal. Immediately she said, 'Oh, not another nurse! I do hope you can do this, the last nurse put the eyes back cross-ways!'

I assured her that there wasn't a problem and very, very, carefully I got on with the job – a little planning beforehand was all that was necessary. As I worked I chatted to her; she was a healthy, intelligent woman. Apparently she had had a growth removed behind the eyes; her sight couldn't be saved, and the eyes had to be removed. She had been blind for a number of years. She lived alone and I was amazed at her cheery disposition. Providing everything was returned to its original place, she could look after herself, while a kindly neighbour did her weekly shopping.

I decided that district nursing was rewarding and the cases I nursed in their own homes were proof that many 'sickies' could live as normal a life as possible with a daily visit and a little help.

There were times when in my room I would think of the 'big house', Rabbit Pit Cottage and my school days and will always remember the smile on the headmistress's face when I said that I would be a nurse one day. Having proved the medical superintendent wrong when he had said I was 'hopeless', I had a little giggle – I had proved them all wrong. Who said it couldn't be done? With sheer guts and willpower many jobs could be done. I was very happy in my chosen career.

CHAPTER 18

Muriel was a wonderful nurse and, like me, enjoyed the challenge of nursing patients in their own homes. No matter what cropped up, she would cope. At first I was concerned about how she would avoid the tram lines on her district. Laughingly she told how they attracted her like a magnet. Many times she got stuck in them and fell off; she would sit between them with the bike on top of her. Fortunately, except for torn stockings and a few bruises, she escaped serious injury, and eventually became an expert on that trusty bike.

Her cases were similar to mine, and one morning she found a patient lying on the floor. She had been there for some time. Apparently she had knelt down to clean out her small fireplace, then found that owing to her arthritis she couldn't get up. Muriel took over this chore for her, always arriving early to do it.

It wasn't unusual to see dead rabbits hanging from her handle bars. Her area being round the city, she had access to the shops. Seeing the rabbits on a 'special' she would take them to house-bound patients, who were very grateful. Often she would return to the nurses' home with home baked goodies which we gratefully enjoyed. The meals at the home were meagre and certainly not very attractive. For one evening meal I remember we had sausages, or I should say 'sausage', because there was only one each. There was one left on the big dish, and it looked very lonely. No one spoke, then Matron warned us that we mustn't waste food. 'Think of the boys on the Burma Road,' she said. We all wanted that sausage but no one was game to say so and our eyes followed it as it was taken to the kitchen. The snacks we had in our bedroom kept us going, but there was little we could buy in war-time as we had to have coupons.

Muriel, told the story of her involvement with a policeman during her evening round. At about nine o'clock she was cycling to one of her patients when out of the gloom a deep voice boomed out, 'Just a minute, pull over.'

She went over to him and, recognising him in his uniform, she said, 'What's the problem, officer?'

'Oh it's you, nurse, it's your bike light, it's a bit bright, let me have a look at it.' The black-out was in force and the bicycle lights were partially covered with black adhesive tape. 'It's OK, nurse,' he said with a chuckle, 'I suppose you are busy.'

'Flat out,' said Muriel as she pedalled away, but called out as she did so, 'Officer, don't tell me I haven't got a rear light – I already know.'

Very little worried her and her cheeky personality got her out of many sticky situations.

Cycling down the hill one day her brakes failed and she went through an intersection very fast, with her uniform billowing behind her; she was told that she looked like the flying nun. She was very lucky to avoid injury. We both had many narrow misses on our bikes. Were unseen forces at work, did we have guardian angels? We liked to think so.

Newspapers were a great asset and we always carried some in our bags. We would use them to cover the table when preparing to do a dressing. For sterilisation we would pack a small biscuit tin with gauge cotton wool, etc., and ask the patient to bake it in the oven for a little while. This was a little job that the patients were always willing to do and it proved very successful.

Ulcers on the legs of many of the elderly patients were nasty things to heal. One of my cases, a woman in her seventies, had a big one on her leg which had been there for a long time. Conscientiously, I carried out doctor's treatment daily but as soon as I left she would take off my dressing and use her own favourite ointment, in which she had great faith. There was little I could do except tell her I was well aware what she was doing, and had to let it go at that. It didn't heal but it didn't get any worse either.

What a variety of cases we met as district nurses! There was never a dull moment but there were some great challenges.

Leaving a house one day I was surprised to find three grubby children standing near my bicycle. One grinned at me and said, 'Have you got a baby in that bag, nurse?'

'Not today,' I replied. 'It's much too cold.'

It wasn't a very sensible answer, but how could I explain the facts of life to those three children? Consoling myself, I felt assured that they would learn very quickly and hopefully in a nice way. My mother had told me I was found under a cabbage leaf, and I spent a lot of time looking.

How things have changed! These days young children are taught the facts of life at an early age. While I'm not against this, I would suggest that it should depend on the individual child and that one should only answer questions truthfully when asked. One has to ask oneself if a small child can absorb so much at such an early age. I don't think so. The early years of innocence can be so easily destroyed.

One morning a call came for me to attend Mrs Miller who had had a slight stroke. On arrival I could hardly see her; she was in a single bed in the corner of the room, surrounded by so much furniture. I prepared to give her a blanket bath, but what a shock I got when turning back the bed clothes – the poor woman was covered with bugs. I told her daughter, who asked me to keep my voice down as she didn't want the neighbours to know. Her mother was very difficult and when she had moved in, she wanted to bring everything with her. I could understand how sad it would be to give up the pieces she had loved.

I immediately reported back to the home and returned with the supervisor, and dressed in gowns we got Mrs Miller out of bed and sat her in a chair wrapped in a rug. The bed clothes were taken out to the backyard. We cleaned the bed with disinfectant. Her daughter provided another mattress and clean bed clothes. Sadly, most of the furniture was removed. Mrs Miller was then bathed and put to bed. Not a word was spoken while this was going on. Her daughter assured us the rest of the room would be inspected and that her husband would wash down the walls. Giving Mrs Miller a drink, I wished her 'Goodbye,' to which she replied, 'Thank you, my dear, God bless yer, but don't come tomorrow.'

I continued my daily visits. She was a spritely old lady and I didn't see any more bugs. She made a complete recovery and it wasn't unusual to see her making her way to the local pub for her glass of ale.

Most evenings were spent writing reports. Some cases should have been in hospital but it was their choice to remain at home, which made the nursing care sometimes very difficult. We visited some patients twice a day and sometimes there was a request from a doctor for us to visit someone in his care. This was no effort on our part, because they were always pleased to see us.

After we had been there four months our future was discussed. We were presented with a four-year contract which we were expected to sign if we wished to train as midwives. Not having been told of this beforehand, and having completed a four-year contract at the London Hospital, we didn't wish to sign for another four years. It was with much regret that we had to leave. We loved the district nursing and the patients; it was such rewarding work. As I said to Muriel, 'It was my cup of tea.'

We were accepted to do midwifery in Leicester, another beautiful city which hadn't been ravaged by the war except for the dropping of an occasional land-mine. It was noted for its medieval churches and architectural features. There were also some lovely gardens, but the many council estates were overcrowded and run down.

We spend a few days with Muriel's parents before commencing to study in the world of midwifery.

CHAPTER 19

The maternity hospital was not a modern building but was adequate. I believe that at one stage it had been two houses.

As pupil midwives we soon settled in. We were told of our responsibilities. This involved caring for the woman after admission and following through until she was discharged. We had to do ten deliveries, writing up each one in detail. As there were other pupil midwives we each took turns, so everyone was on call.

Witnessing the birth of a baby was a big thrill, as was each baby I delivered. The actual birth for some women was slow and painful, and I asked myself why that was so. Surely it could have been easier – but there was no choice, and for some women it was a pain they never forgot.

It was always hoped that the baby would arrive head first, the normal way, but there were times when it was a breech presentation with bottom first. The woman was monitored at all times and any abnormalities were quickly noted. I loved the excitement and the joy of handing Mum her baby, and accepted the birth of a baby as a normal function for the woman.

Very soon our time was up and how quickly it had passed! It had been a rewarding six months and we felt confident that we would be able to cope with the following six months, which were to be spent in the surrounding district. After a few days' break in which we crammed in a lot of study, we sat for the exam. We had no trouble in passing, and it was time to move on and present ourselves to the midwife who was to teach us the ups and downs of delivering babies in the home.

On being introduced to the midwife for my area I was surprised to see she really looked the part – buxom, she had a round chubby face and she oozed confidence. Her name was Miss Jones and it appeared she had dedicated her life to being a midwife.

I was billeted with a milkman and his wife in a modest home which was very comfortable. Mrs Till didn't look particularly well and I noticed the early signs of multiple sclerosis. They were very kind to me and in spite of the rationing, I was well fed. She said she was unable to have children and I thought this was sad as she would have made a good mother. I didn't see much of Mr Till, who was always coming and going.

As pupil midwives we always took the first call and the midwife would follow later. It was a great responsibility, with some nervous tension at the start. Mrs Till, my hostess, always heard the knock on the door first, no matter what time it was, and during the night the sound of the window being raised would waken me. She would then call out in a loud voice, 'Did you want the midwife? Hang on, I'll get her.' By that time I was up and dressed, well aware that the neighbours would know that I was called out to a case.

Some homes were most unsuitable for home confinements, but we just did out best and no one was turned away.

The midwife carried a small machine called the 'Minuet's Apparatus', which was a great asset. During a contraction the woman would hold the mask on her face to breathe the gas. It was self-administered, but quite safe to use, because as she became sleepy, she would let the mask slip, then would become sufficiently alert to use the mask again. We learnt how to use this and had to pass an exam.

I hadn't seen Mother for some time. She had a male friend, which I thought was an excellent idea, but I didn't like his way of life. He drank and his language was appalling. They had a few fights but they managed to survive. I was told he was a cook in the army. Mother had been living in Leicester for a while and I'm not sure why she had made this move. The home, which was at the back of a shop, was quite comfortable. There were two floors and plenty of room. It was in my area and I was able to pop in quite often. As I was in uniform, it set the neighbour's tongues wagging. One approached Mother to ask how she was, as she said she had seen the midwife call. Mother didn't enlighten her so I should think she was a very puzzled neighbour. Both my brothers were in the army. I heard from them occasionally, but they said very little and I never heard where they were.

Many amusing incidents happened as I cycled round the district as a midwife. One woman had left it a little late in calling me – it was her seventh baby. On arrival, I could see that the birth was imminent. I told her to rest her right leg on my shoulder. (We had been taught to deliver on the side for better control of the head, also to prevent a tear of the perineum.)

There had been no time to take off my hat and coat, and my hat was held on my head with a large hat pin, as sometimes the bow under the chin would slip. She gave a yell as the pin had stuck in her leg. She knocked off my hat just as baby's head was born; alas, baby was born wearing my hat! Oh! to have had a camera. I think she would remember this incident and tell the child, when she was able to understand, how she had been born wearing the midwife's hat.

It was a busy life and we were very lucky to get an uninterrupted night's sleep. I went to bed early when I was able. The days and nights were cold and I loathed leaving my warm bed.

It was 1.30 one night when I heard Mrs Till say, 'I'll get her.' How lovely it would have been to roll over – such luxury! I yawned and dressed quickly, and didn't recognise the anxious man waiting. He didn't speak as he carried my bag. We trudged in the snow which had fallen and had made it a white scene. I hadn't met his wife, which was worrying as I didn't know what to expect. Hoping for the best, it was a consoling thought that Sister Jones wasn't far away. There was always a doctor on call should he be needed, but we didn't worry him very much.

The house felt warm as we entered and, as it was a council house, I knew its layout. I took off my hat and coat and went upstairs. Mrs Smith was sitting on the bed and I could see she was well advanced in labour. There was a small coal fire burning in the grate and a butcher's basket nearby, which was to be used as a bassinet. The double bed looked clean and comfortable; in fact, the room was clean and tidy – always a big plus!

At the age of thirty years, Mrs Smith appeared withdrawn and was very nervous, and I had the feeling that she was dominated by her husband. This was her second pregnancy and her son aged seven years was asleep in his bedroom. She said he was her pride and joy. As I examined her I questioned her as to why she hadn't attended antenatal clinic; she said her husband didn't think it was necessary. Anyway, he brought us a cup of tea which was most acceptable.

In spite of the fire burning in the grate, it was cold. The patient made good progress and at 2.35 I delivered a baby girl. She gave a lusty cry and looked healthy, but I was puzzled as Mrs Smith was rather big in pregnancy and this baby was so small. I told her that she had a lovely little daughter, but that she was very tiny.

'Just roll over on to your back,' I told her, 'so that I can listen to your tummy.'

My fears were confirmed – here was a multiple birth.

'Are there any twins in your family?' I asked.

'My Gawd, no,' she said.

'I'll ask your hubby to get the other midwife as there is another little one in there.'

Standing at the top of the stairs, I told him what was happening and the poor man rushed out of the house as if he were being chased. A cry from the bed jolted me back from my thoughts. I couldn't believe what I was seeing – a small foot showing!

As calmly as I could, I explained what was happening, reassuring her that there was no problem and that Sister Jones would be along shortly, but in the meantime I would need her help. Gently I pushed the foot back and told her to pant really hard when she got a contraction as we didn't want the baby to be born too quickly. She co-operated very well and hung grimly to the towel I had wrapped around the bedhead. Gradually the little baby was born. I wrapped a towel round and, speaking to Mrs Smith, I said, 'Now really pant hard when the next contraction starts – baby's head must also be born very slowly.'

All the time, I was hoping to see Sister Jones' chubby face joining me. The baby's head was born with no problem – another little girl. She cried well and I labelled her number 2 and put her to join number 1 in the butcher's basket. The after birth followed soon after, and Mrs Smith didn't need sutures. I congratulated her and said those two dear little girls would be in good hands. I don't believe she heard me; there were tears in her eyes as she looked at her babies.

While making her comfortable, I heard Sister Jones' cheery voice coming up the stairs, followed by the frantic husband, then a very sleepy little boy who had been disturbed by the noise. The babies were bathed and they were like two peas in a pod; one weighed four pounds and the other one four pounds one ounce. After a cup of tea and a lot of 'oh's' and 'ah's', we went home. Sister Jones kindly drove me. I didn't undress but I lay on the bed because I would be up and about very shortly. I was content, my prayers had been answered. All had gone well. I kept in touch with Mrs Smith for a short time. As I predicted, she was a wonderful mother and her twins were beautiful.

My midwife was well experienced; she never raised her voice and was extremely kind. She was an excellent teacher. Her car was her problem as it was an erratic starter and there were times when we had to push it.

Each delivery had to be written up in detail and in all there were twenty. I found this part of the course was so time-consuming.

Most babies seem to arrive in the early hours of the morning but one call did come in at 10 a.m. I arrived to find some of the neighbours congregated in the bedroom. I never did see the husband – it looked like a mother's meeting with such a babble of noise. Some of the women were quite chubby and I wasn't sure which was the expectant mother. Eventually, one by one, they left the room. As I examined Mrs Grey, she told me she was thirty-five years old and that her daughter was ten years old but in between she had had three miscarriages so this birth would be very special. After making sure there was someone I could call if I needed help, I prepared her for the birth.

When I needed to go to the toilet, she suggested I use the bucket in the corner of the room, as the toilet was out the back. She giggled as she said, 'We're all girls together.' I didn't use the bucket.

She made good progress but when the baby's head was born, it was very blue. This prompted me to suspect the cord was round the neck, and my suspicions were confirmed. I was able to get my fingers under, then I used my forceps to clamp the cord but unfortunately that pair snapped. I hastily cut the cord as the baby had to be born as soon as possible. It was a little boy and I gave a sigh of relief as he turned pink after a lusty cry. Mum was ecstatic. In no time at all I made her comfortable then dashed out to the back to use the toilet. Coming back, I found a cup of tea waiting and the neighbours were back crowding the room.

It didn't take long to deliver my quota of twenty babies, each one a delight. Muriel had done the same. We were both so busy that I didn't see much of her. It had been a wonderful experience, we had met some fine people and, of course, our 'mums'. Our records, which were conscientiously kept, were graded 'excellent' and we agreed that we had been well taught.

The war continued but there was very little air activity during that twelve months spent in Leicester, though the coastal areas were still getting bombed regularly.

It was a sad parting when I said goodbye to Mrs Till and her milkman husband, as I had been so well cared for. No matter what time I arrived back from a case, even at midnight, she was there for me.

Before the exam we went home to Coventry for a few days to stay with Muriel's parents. Walking was a great pastime and we studied as we went along, throwing questions at one another.

The day for the exam arrived and, of course, we were anxious. As we changed into uniform we sang 'The Laughing Song', much to the amazement of the other candidates who thought we were mad. We were pleased with our effort and were hopeful of passing well.

I had kept in touch with Matron of the London Hospital and she invited us to return. I don't believe the nurses' board in Leicester was too impressed with our decision, as we were told they had many openings for us to practise as midwives.

Receiving our results, we were pleased to see that we had passed well. Not only was I a 'State Registered Nurse', I was now a 'State Certified Midwife'.

CHAPTER 20

In a way, it was like going home. Another move and I thought of the many my parents had made but I was certain now that Mother would stay put in Leicester; she was coping well.

An interview with Matron at the London Hospital saw us both in the midwifery section. I went on the district and Muriel in the ward. On the district we were six, sister-in-charge, and five qualified midwives. The area round the hospital was well covered, a one mile radius. It was policy that no one was turned away, everyone was given treatment should they need it, and there were a number of midwifery cases who had not booked. There was always an obstetrician on call. We walked, caught a bus or travelled on the underground.

The East End hadn't changed much and most of the streets were covered with rubble, with some buildings just a shell. In most streets there was an air-raid shelter but I always hurried past; to me they always looked so menacing, although it was unheard of that anyone in London Hospital uniform had been attacked.

We took turns to be on call, and the hall porter would ring our rooms if we were needed. When called, we were soon up as we were experts at throwing our clothes on. One night, it being my turn, I went to the front hall where I found a man who was nervously waiting. He took my bag but walked so fast I had to run to keep up with him. He lived in a tenement building on the fourth floor. It was very dark, there being no lights; he kept lighting matches and as we went up the stairs, I hung on to his coat as I stumbled after him.

The flat was very bare but there was no time to look round – a very blue little baby was lying between the mother's legs on top of the bed clothes. There wasn't any heat in the flat but there was a fire place. Throwing on some bits of wood, then covering it with some kerosene, the husband put a match to it. It went up with a whoosh – frightening me – it

85

wasn't a very sensible thing to do. It was a messy clean up and as soon as the kettle boiled, I bathed the baby who responded well to the warmth. That small kettle was heated many times, and it was a slow process.

The fire burned slowly as I worked. They said they had just moved in and that their three children were in the other room. Not a sound had they made. The cleaning done, we had the usual cuppa. I said that I would be back later and would bring some clothes for the children, as the hospital had a stock which had been generously donated. Never a dull moment being a midwife!

One evening on my way to visit a family I was stopped by a man who said he wanted to take me home with him. It was very dark and I expect he was confused and hadn't recognised my uniform. He smelt strongly of drink. He put his arm round me but I pushed him away. I gripped my 'smutter bag' harder. In this bag we carried a small bed mackintosh, newspaper, old linen, etc – anything we might need for the confinement. It was quite heavy and swinging it would give the receiver an almighty 'whack'. The delivery bag was a closed bag; the contents had been sterilised. So it was with these two bags that we trudged to our cases. After a while I was able to convince the man who I was and he then offered to carry my bag. I didn't give him this but walked on. He followed for a while but I soon left him behind.

On Christmas Eve, it was my turn again – it would be, and a party was in progress. I danced with the obstetrician, who was a good dancer, but I was flat-footed. He asked who was on call and when I told him I was, apparently he was too. He laughingly threatened me, saying, 'Don't you dare call me.' I thought 'Big deal for you.' We went on dancing. It was a good party, as everyone seemed to be letting their hair down, hoping there would be no interruptions from Hitler's bombs.

The call came in at about 11.30 and as I left the room, I turned and waved to the doctor who shook his fist at me. I was very fond of that young man and I knew he had feelings for me also, but I had to hold my emotions in check. How could I take friends to meet my mother and her new husband? They had been married for a few weeks, and I wasn't invited to the ceremony. Definitely not. Looking back over the years, I should not have been so worried as to what they did and how they lived; I should have relaxed and lived my own life but I found that so difficult.

I arrived at the tenement building, and trudged up the stairs. The mother greeted me with a toothless grin; she was well advanced in labour, and she cheerfully said it was her ninth. Immediately I asked if she usually had to have stitches after her babies were born.

'My Gawd, yes,' she chuckled. 'I'm usually torn from Damn to Bethsheba, but the good old doc always patches me up pretty well.'

'Well,' I thought to myself, 'Look out, doc, you're going to be needed.'

Having babies didn't worry her – she was a happy soul. Well, I tried and sadly watched the tear as baby's head was born; she certainly needed stitches. I sent hubby for the doctor. In the meantime I told the mother of my conversation with the doctor. 'He said he would strangle me if I called him, so when he comes, I'll hide under the bed.'

She enjoyed the joke. This I did as he came up the stair.

'Where is she?' he asked in a loud voice.

Poking my head out from under the bed, I laughed as I said, 'Are you looking for me?'

We enjoyed the situation but it had been very messy under that bed; I don't think it had been cleaned for months. Doctor said he would wait for me and that he would go downstairs to chat to the old man.

The baby, a lovely little boy, was ready for a feed. I asked if she planned more but she just grinned, saying, 'Gawd knows.'

We drove back to the hospital and as I sat beside him I thought how wonderful he was, and every now and then he would look at me, and my heart turned somersaults. We didn't speak and on arrival we parted company.

One evening, Muriel was off duty and as I wasn't on call, we decided to go for a walk. We did a lot of talking about how we had come a long way since Tredegar House, both of us agreeing that midwifery and district nursing were exciting and rewarding. We laughed as we remembered the rabbits hanging from her handlebars, the episode with the policeman, the goodies we brought back and enjoyed in our room. I thought of Charles with sadness – such a loss! Choosing to walk behind the hospital, there was a delicious smell of fish and chips. Can anything taste better even though they were wrapped in newspaper? We were able to buy just a few. There was a lull in the air activity, but occasionally the powerful searchlights picked up a plane in the sky. We accepted the possibility of bombs falling, but somehow it didn't worry us.

Hearing footsteps behind, we turned to find a policeman following us. As we were not in uniform, he wouldn't have recognised us.

'What are you two young ladies up to?' he asked.

'Just going for a walk.'

He asked where we were from and when we told him he said, 'This isn't a nice area, I'll walk you back.'

This he did and ate more than his share of the chips.

On the district during the year we were joined by medical students. Having completed their stint in the midwifery ward, they were to learn about home confinements. Some were very good but the young man who accompanied me was a 'know-all'. We had been attending to a woman who was having her first baby. She told us that her husband was a sailor – of course, we didn't always believe what we were told. Dressed in evening wear as he'd been to a dance, but wearing a white cotton gown, he sat in front of her, saying that was the way he liked to deliver the baby. I made no comment but as the baby's head was showing, I suggested it would be a good idea if he ruptured the membranes. He didn't. I knew what would happen, and with the next contraction she pushed hard and the membranes ruptured. It was a bull's eye, he was hit in the face and collected a puddle in his lap. Nothing was said though I felt like commenting, 'I told you so.' It was a normal delivery and a lovely baby but it was a very wet young man who walked back to the hospital with me. Did he learn anything? I hope so.

After seven months on the district I was invited to work in the midwifery department. I did admit to being tired, and now I was to have set hours and definitely would not be on call. I reported on night duty.

The fun started when a mother brought her young daughter in because she complained of tummy pains. Her mother had given her a hot water bottle but as the pains became more constant, she brought her to the hospital. I found it hard to believe that she couldn't see that her daughter was pregnant. Nonetheless, the pregnancy confirmed, she gave her daughter a resounding slap across the face and left her. I could only hope that when she saw her granddaughter she would forgive her.

I remember giving an expectant young woman a bath. She was very talkative and confided that she wasn't exactly sure of her dates. I thought I would be able to help her, so said, 'When did you last menstruate?'

'Oh! No!' she said. 'I'm Church of England.'

The medical students were always up to mischief and early one morning one dressed as an expectant woman. He certainly made a good job of it but as he was helped on to the bed, I spotted a hairy leg. We held him down and gave him a dose of castor oil for his trouble. They were good sports and always ready to help.

A doctor's wife was admitted during the early hours of the morning – she was expecting twins but was six weeks early. She wasn't very happy. Her husband had a commitment that he couldn't ignore. He suggested that maybe it could be a false alarm and that she should rest in bed. Having a full-time housekeeper, he went, leaving a phone number. She wasn't impressed but was delivered of two boys, which were tiny but well developed. I called them Pip and Squeak. Except for needing assistance with feeding they made good progress and she was able to breast feed them both. I got to know her well and when she went home I would visit, as it was only a short bus ride away. The babies made good progress, but her husband died soon afterwards of lung cancer. He was fifty-three years old.

There was more trouble for her as the younger boy was diagnosed as retarded. That was devastating news and it seemed that the problems just piled up. She finally committed suicide and unfortunately I lost touch with the boys. The older of the two by fifteen minutes, in spite of being an asthmatic, was very bright but the other little fellow needed constant attention.

On a lighter note there was the young teenager who came to the outpatient department with tummy ache. She was amazed when told she was pregnant, saying she didn't have a clue how it had happened; then she brightly remarked, 'We did have a bomb in the back garden.'

Queen Mary was president of the London Hospital from 1924. She was a frequent visitor and to reach Matron's flat she would have to pass along the corridor of the midwifery section. As she was likely to drop in at any time, we were told to approach her and curtsy and say, 'Good morning, Ma'am' or 'Good afternoon, Ma'am', whatever time of the day it was. She was very approachable but I could see that she wasn't impressed as I went to greet her with a bedpan in my hand. She suggested that it would be a good idea to put it away. On another occasion I found her talking to the mothers in one of the small wards. As

I approached her she pointed to the corner of the ward, saying, 'Is that dust, nurse, or a shadow?' I was able to tell her that it was a shadow. I never saw her smile. I did meet her on a number of occasions, and she showed interest in all that was going on.

When George VI died, Elizabeth II became patron.

CHAPTER 21

D Day eventually came and in 1945 the war was over. What a great feeling and general relief that was, what excitement as we all celebrated. I had spent the last two months living in a beautiful house in Hertfordshire owned by the Earl of Strathmore. The London Hospital had used it as a maternity hospital for some of the women living in the East End. To them it was a dream, a lovely home, with good food as far as the rations would allow, and beautiful gardens. There was no sign of war, just peaceful countryside. What luxury!

Mostly there were eighteen women with their babies due in two weeks. Usually they stayed another two weeks. While I was there, there were no problems and I wondered if the peaceful surroundings contributed towards that. For entertainment, there were lovely walks, the radio, sing-songs, and every Sunday hymn singing which was enjoyed by all. Two well known actors who lived in the area had a riding school and they would hire out the horses. I soon got involved and was a regular visitor.

At the back of the house two grooms trained racehorses – such beautiful creatures. One day, riding my hack, I met them as they were exercising their horses. They grinned at me, saying, 'You should ride a good horse.'

Cheekily I replied, 'Opportunity would be a fine thing.'

They invited me to join them on my next half day off. I didn't believe this was met with approval by the sister-in-charge, but I loved horses.

Sitting on a racehorse was so different from a hack; I did ask them to lower the stirrups but they wouldn't do that. Nevertheless a slap on the rump and I was away. I had no control whatsoever. I galloped madly across two fields, while I hung on for dear life. Eventually I was able to rein it in and we cantered back to the stables. The grooms were very worried as it was a valuable horse but no damage was done. They said, 'I bet you're not game to ride again?'

'Oh, yes, please,' I said and I did at every opportunity I got! It was wonderful. The horses were trained to race six furlongs. I wondered what my Dad would have said!

Back at the London hospital I met up with Muriel again. We were invited to see Matron. She asked if we would consider doing the sister tutor's course. I immediately said, 'No', but Muriel was very keen. We were given two weeks to think about it; in the meantime we were to be promoted to 'sister' and to wear that lovely blue uniform. How wonderful!

I declined to do the sister tutors' course, but Muriel said she would do it alone. How could I tell her and them that I didn't have the money to pay for the course, as there was very little money in my bank? So for me it was back to the general side of nursing, and leaving the mothers and babies was very sad indeed. Muriel failed the first exam at the college and she was very upset. I was surprised as she was so knowledgeable, but we have always studied together; I felt that I had failed her also. She did resit but again failed. Unfortunately, because she didn't wish to leave the midwifery department to go back to general nursing, she decided to leave. We had been together on and off for ten years, and it was a very sad parting. She wrote later to say that she was night sister in a busy maternity hospital. She was a born midwife.

As junior sister my duties were varied, including checking situations that had nothing at all to do with nursing. At one time I was involved with the laundry, checking that things ran smoothly and changing the towels in all the toilets. I nicknamed myself 'Morsy Bagwash'. During this spell I learnt so much about how the wheels turned to keep the hospital running smoothly.

My sister Dorothy and I had corresponded during my training. Her first marriage had been a disaster, leaving her with one child, a boy, but her second marriage was much more successful, and she had two more boys.

My sister found an uncle in Australia, I never understood how she did this, but I received a letter from him inviting me to visit. It was an attractive offer but firstly I was under contract with the London Hospital – also, I couldn't afford it. We did correspond and I asked lots of questions about the family which he couldn't answer; as far as he was concerned, we had just disappeared.

Amazingly, I also heard from Dad's two sisters. They were well established in business in England. A third aunt contacted me from California. It seemed that all my relatives were coming out of the woodwork. Did I need them now? No, I didn't. They were shattered to hear what had happened to us after we left the big house. Anyway, I couldn't fill in the missing pieces of the jigsaw puzzle and so I suggested that we forget the past.

John was now out of the army and although he was offered his old job back he couldn't settle. He did eventually marry and have a family and lived in Leicester.

My aunt in California had had four sons but unfortunately two were killed during the war. She was very keen for me to visit, but I had decided that in about six month's time I would go to Australia.

Life went on. I enjoyed wandering round the hospital filling in where needed; then I was the relieving sister in the wards. This was a real challenge and I had to be on my toes at all times. The short time I spent relieving in the children's ward I found very difficult. In my charge was a four-day-old baby who had had a tracheotomy, a girl Elizabeth with TB meningitis and a seven-year-old who had had a brain tumour which had been difficult to find. This child had been passed over as a spoilt child, with her symptoms attributed to that. When she was admitted her mother told me how she had gone from doctor to doctor and she was very frustrated. The child did look reasonably well. She had been admitted for observation and the many tests eventually showed the brain tumour. The operation was a success, the tumour was completely removed and she made good progress. Her parents were so relieved. They told me they had four other children and how could they have possibly spoilt that child? I was very pleased to move to another ward. Caring for sick babies and children could be very depressing; it had to be a very special person to be able to do that. I know I shed a few tears.

It was time to book my passage by sea to Australia, and on making inquiries and because of my qualifications I was told I could travel as a migrant, but that I would have to go to Australia House for information. This I did and was delighted to hear that I would be accepted and the cost involved would be ten pounds. This was hard to believe and certainly well within my pocket. I had to produce a medical certificate, then sat back and waited for my ticket.

The last few weeks I spent at an annexe of the hospital in Surrey, a place where the patients were able to relax and recover in lovely surroundings. I relaxed also – it was great.

On Tuesday evening we had a short service and the young curate was Bill, a tall blond young man who was very popular. We became very friendly and I joined him after the service to drive to the local pub where he had many friends, and also round the parish. Collecting for the blind, one day I went to the vicarage and was met by an elderly man, the vicar, who looked at me over his glasses, asking, 'Who might you be?'

When I told him, he said, 'Oh, you're the one who is corrupting my curate.'

'Not so,' I said laughingly, though I did find him very attractive.

I had notified Matron of my intention to go to Australia and, having completed my contract of two years, I was pleased when my ticket arrived. There was much to do, so many people to farewell; I told them it was only for a holiday and to visit relatives. Not wanting goodbyes at the boat train, Bill insisted he came with me. He gave me a beautiful fountain pen, wished me luck and said, 'Keep in touch.'

It was goodbye, England – but I'll be back.

CHAPTER 22

It was 8 July, 1948. I looked at the huge ship docked at Southampton. It was called *Austurias*, and I reminded myself that this ship was to be my home for the next few weeks.

I joined the other passengers going up the gangway. I couldn't say they looked jubilant; no doubt they were feeling as apprehensive as I was. It was a big step to take. There were many rumours about Australia; apparently the aborigines weren't happy about the influx of the white settlers. I understood that they were the original nomadic inhabitants. The last letter I had received from my uncle in Melbourne stated that he had got rid of the chooks (we called them chickens) and had white-washed the shed. He hoped that I would be comfortable living there.

I leaned on the rail watching some passengers saying their weepy 'goodbyes', and although at my request there was no one to wave 'goodbye' to me, I wept also.

A small woman standing next to me was crying bitterly; she looked at me with my hair blowing in the breeze and said, 'Put this scarf around your head – you will get a cold.' She would have been in her early fifties and was travelling with her husband Bert and daughter Doreen. Little did I realise that she was to play a big part in my future. We went down to our cabin which was on the third deck, to find our luggage there, and I was pleased to find that I was to share a cabin with them. The husbands were to sleep lower down in the ship, and I thought this was sad. Meeting Bert later, I noticed that he had the loveliest smiling brown eyes; no wonder he had produced such an attractive daughter in Doreen. 'Frostie,' as she was called, told me that they were travelling to Geelong in Victoria to join Bert's brother, Ted, who was a widower.

The cabin was small for eight adult women. There were two handbasins, but the bathrooms and toilets were down the corridor. They were basic but adequate.

I chose an upper bunk; below me was a lass who hadn't been married very long and was pregnant, as I found out later. Poor dear, she was having difficulty coping with morning sickness. She spent the days with her husband. Opposite also on the upper bunk was a very unhappy woman. She had a fear of the sea and was very apprehensive about the trip. I didn't learn much about her, but was pleased to hear that she wasn't travelling alone. She was sick before we left port and I thought what a miserable trip she could look forward to. Most of the time she spent lying on her bunk.

The lower bunk was taken up by 'Blondie'; it wasn't easy to guess her age but she was a happy person, always on the go. She was very excited at the prospect of travelling to Australia to live with relatives and like me she was travelling alone. The next two bunks were Frostie and daughter Doreen, and at the far end another mother and daughter. What a mixed bunch we were in that small cabin, but surprisingly we got on very well and we all hoped we had done the right thing. The challenge of the sea was inviting, the elements so unpredictable. What challenges lay ahead?

I had heard that the *Austurias* was very old, and that it had been a troop ship during the war. The sitting rooms were spacious and tastefully decorated; in fact, on the whole the ship was very comfortable. I believe there were about two thousand passengers, most of them migrants, and the many children were well catered for.

We sailed on 9 July, and the ship groaned and shuddered as it was guided out to sea. We passed Cowes, Portsmouth, Ventnor and then into the English Channel. The water was calm and we took this opportunity to explore. There were the games room, billiards, deck quoits and swimming and with the promise of excellent meals, the trip had a potential for enjoyment.

We were only two days out when some passengers complained of tummy-ache. This was expected but didn't last long. There was a dance that night and I was beginning to enjoy myself. Eventually we anchored off Gibraltar and from a distance it looked like a very large rock sticking up out of the ocean. We were not allowed ashore, but small boats came alongside to sell their goodies. I bought a scarf.

Frostie mothered us. She had bought a teapot, tea and sugar, and it was lovely to be offered an early morning cup of tea. What a busy bee she was! She confided to me that she was very apprehensive about her decision to leave home. She was also worried about Doreen as she was always being surrounded by admirers. I thought that Doreen was able to take care of herself, but that I would keep an eye on her during the trip.

A meeting was held among the passengers to discuss the possibility of having a concert. Volunteers were asked for ideas, also to take part and, not being shy in making a fool of myself, I said I would do a monologue. Some of the passengers played musical instruments which they had brought with them; this was a wonderful asset and together they formed a band. There was a great excitement and it seemed that everyone wanted to get into the act, so plans were made for rehearsals. On 14 July we passed Sicily, off the coast of Italy. It was smooth sailing.

I heard of a passenger who at great cost had brought her two dogs with her. Unfortunately she wasn't too happy about the care they were given and said so. During the night they disappeared – apparently they were thrown overboard. That was the conclusion, because they disappeared. She was absolutely devastated. What a dreadful thing to do! I felt sick thinking of those little dogs swimming to nowhere and eventually drowning. A feeling of gloom spread over the ship, but the person responsible was never found.

The Mediterranean was lovely and it was very warm when we reached Port Said about 6.40 p.m. on 17 July. The Arabs swarmed round the ship like bees round a honey pot, with the aid of the ship's lights and lanterns. I didn't buy anything.

It took ten hours to sail through the Suez Canal, and what an incredible trip that was! It was so narrow that the ship seemed only just to fit. We could have almost shaken hands with those on the banks. Some of the locals showed off by exposing themselves but, except for a few giggles, no one really took much notice. We then continued to the entrance of the Red Sea, which proved to be a very interesting part of the trip. It was extremely hot and uncomfortable, but the mountain scenery was magnificent.

In the cabin we fitted in very well. I was sorry for the lass on the upper bunk, where she stayed for most of the time. I did my best to help her, saying she would feel better if she moved around, but all she wanted to do was to get off the ship. The comedian in the cabin was Blondie. She must have been in her late forties but she certainly enjoyed life, and also her tot of cherry brandy every now and then. One evening we had settled down for the night, when about eleven o'clock there was a roar from Blondie, 'Look at the buggers,' she yelled. 'Queuing up to be killed.' She was hitting cockroaches with the heel of her shoe.

The sea continued calm, the weather warm and sunny, and we were still getting to know one another. Getting ready for bed one evening I couldn't help but notice that one of the women had a small growth hanging from her inner thigh. This puzzled me somewhat as the person was definitely female, but then one never knows! One day I found her alone in the cabin and we got talking. I told her that I had seen the growth, and that I had wondered about it. She was very embarrassed as she told me that it had started as a very small ball, 'as big as my thumb-nail,' she said. It hung from a thread, like a piece of string, and it had grown to the size of a golf ball. Obviously the thread was a small tube or blood vessel that was feeding the growth.

'How did you get past the medical?' I asked her.

'They never looked there,' she said. My medical was very thorough, and I wondered how the doctor had overlooked this. I advised her to get it checked as soon as possible.

'It will only be a simple operation; if you ignore it, it will continue to grow,' I told her.

She seemed happy that she had been able to talk about it and said that it really was a nuisance. I was able to reassure Frostie that we didn't have a man in the cabin, and was not a bit surprised to hear that the others had seen it too. I didn't get to know this passenger's daughter very well, but I gathered she was a handful. She wore contact lenses although I think they were more often on the floor than in her eyes.

Mixing with the passengers, I was surprised to learn that one had gone to the same school as I had. His name was John and he was going to Queensland to visit his sister. He knew my sister Dorothy – what a small world it is! He loved music and played the violin, and we spent a good deal of time together. An unknown admirer had tried to attract my attention by throwing sweets into my lap when I was sitting on a deck chair. He was tall, thin and very good-looking. One day I decided to talk to him and maybe cool his ardour somewhat because I wasn't interested. He told me that he was a builder and that he hoped to settle in Melbourne to start his own business. I met him once again one evening on the upper deck; his intentions were obvious but this wasn't for me so I avoided him.

On 22 July we arrived at Aden and it was very hot. We were allowed ashore, although it didn't look very inviting. With John and another young couple we took a taxi, as Aden was some distance from port. It was a most unpleasant trip and I couldn't believe what I saw. The buildings, such as they were, were neglected and dirty; there were no windows, and pigs, goats and chickens wandered at their leisure. The residents were lying in the gutter sleeping. I asked myself whether the houses were for the animals. We looked at the market, which was a round building with stalls inside but we couldn't see the food and fruit for flies. It was a horrible sight. It was depressing to see so many children crippled and under-fed. They begged for money for anything. What could we do? We couldn't help – it was obviously their way of life. We couldn't get back to the ship soon enough, but getting a taxi proved difficult as the driver demanded double the fare and refused to take us unless we paid up. I was getting worried but thankfully John handled the situation and we were very soon back on deck. I told Frostie how horrible it was there, and she was pleased that she hadn't gone.

CHAPTER 23

The following day the sea was very rough; there was a huge swell, and we were warned that a gale was imminent. The ship developed a very exciting roll and walking was difficult – we looked as if we had been on a binge. Some passengers were apprehensive and many were sick, including me.

It was that night that we were to perform the concert. I handed programmes to the passengers as they filed in, and what a relief it was to see Doreen. I felt so sick and literally threw the programmes to her as I rushed to the toilet to be violently sick.

'Will you be able to take part,' she asked, handing back the programmes on my return.

'Oh yes,' I said, 'Why not?'

The concert was a great success, but it was difficult and amusing to try to stand in one spot, with the ship rolling. The concert was to be repeated later. John led the band playing his violin, and throughout the trip he was kept busy playing for dancing and other entertainments. I could listen to him all the time, I too loved music.

The gale lasted twenty-four hours. My little friend on the opposite upper bunk was frantic, and she was given a sedative. There was some crockery broken but very little else and we were very pleased to be coasting along once again in calm waters. During the night a member of the crew died, followed also by a male passenger. He was oldish and had suffered from a heart condition. Both were buried at sea and the service, which was conducted by the captain, was very moving.

I did a spot of baby-sitting for a young couple. Their baby, a lovely little fellow, was nine months old. As there were two seatings for meals, it enabled them to have their meals in peace.

On 28 July we reached Colombo and were allowed ashore. The main street, which was cluttered with shops, was beautifully clean, and well stocked with reasonably cheap goods. One advertised tea that could be sent to England, or to anywhere it seemed. Frostie and I thought this a wonderful idea as Ceylon tea was noted for its taste and quality worldwide. We ordered some to be sent to the family in England and we paid the bill. It never arrived and we were so disappointed; there was no way of checking so there wasn't anything we could do. I wonder how many other people had been so conned. Continuing on our way, we crossed the equator.

The following day was a fancy dress party for the children. What clever mothers they were to produce such a variety of fancy dress at short notice. Their imagination ran riot with clowns and fairies, who appeared suddenly as if by magic.

On 5 August, we arrived at Fremantle – what a lovely city! It was clean with very wide streets. Frostie had friends living there and arrangements had been made to meet. I was pleased to be asked to tag along. It felt good to be on land again, and what a lovely reunion it was! Apparently they had been neighbours in London for a very long time, before migrating to Australia. I just sat listening – what a lot of chatter! But time was on the wing and we had to get back to the ship. They promised to keep in touch and there was a hint that they might consider joining them in Geelong.

Waiting for a taxi Frostie suddenly had an acute attack of gastritis and looked very ill. We were pleased to get back to the ship, and after making her comfortable, I asked if the doctor could see her. He agreed that it was acute gastritis. She soon recovered, but we did miss our early morning cuppa.

We continued through the Australian Bight which had a reputation of being unpredictable but it was very kind to us and there were no mishaps. The entertainment continued – we danced until midnight and the night before we arrived, we had a party in the cabin. It was a lovely evening, but a little sad as we were to go our separate ways. What a great experience it had been! Four weeks on the sea. In my opinion we had been well looked after but, being the busy person I am, I found it a little too long. How could one possibly complain? All this for the cost of ten pounds – it was unbelievable.

We exchanged addresses and I said I would visit Frostie and family in Geelong if at all possible. John was going to Queensland; I had enjoyed his company and his music very much. I had spotted my secret admirer jotting down my address from my luggage, which was on the upper deck with others, but I never heard from him.

I was to stay in Melbourne and wondered whether I really would have to sleep in the chook-shed. Very soon I was to find out.

Getting off the ship, I stood on Australian soil. It was 9 August 1948 and I was thirty years old. Was I ready for Australia? Was Australia ready for me? I was prepared to stay for two years so I would certainly find out. For me it was another challenge.

CHAPTER 24

Standing by my luggage, I looked around. Melbourne was a busy port, thronged with people. Then I spotted them. How could I not recognise my uncle who was so like my Dad in stature? It was quite uncanny. Auntie looked lovely and she was very smartly dressed. I did so want them to like me and I knew I would do my best to make this happen.

We picked up the luggage to take to the car. It was a yellow Morris Cowley and it had a dicky seat at the back. I had only seen one of these cars in a picture book. Nevertheless the luggage was strapped in the dicky seat and we squeezed in the front.

Very little was said as we drove along a very busy road. Surprisingly, the trams took up most of it, and I was told they had the right of way at all times.

Auntie and Uncle were in their seventies but didn't look it. They lived in a modest home in St. Kilda. As we walked down the side entrance we were greeted with loud squawking which came from their cockatoo, a pet they had had for a number of years. He had a large cage at the back door, which was his sleeping quarters, but a fine chain was tied to one of his feet which allowed him to move around. I was amused at his antics and especially when he opened the kitchen door to join us.

The chook pen turned out to be a lovely room with a large double bed.

Uncle had been an electrical engineer before he retired. He had been brought to Australia by Otis. Auntie was his second wife and with a twinkle in his eye he told me that whilst visiting Tasmania where she lived, they had been on a picnic. She made the most delicious sandwiches so he decided that he would marry her. He had three children from his first marriage, one girl and two boys, but only one boy from this union. Unfortunately Wally, as he was named, had medical problems and he never reached his full potential. Mentally he was very alert and very bright and was able to cope very well in a private school. I was told that he had been very excited at the prospect of meeting me and showing me round Melbourne, but unfortunately, three months before I arrived, he had died from a severe haemorrhage from the liver. He was sixteen years old. I could imagine how devastated they were and I hoped that my arrival would help to fill the gap.

Auntie had a part-time job in one of the big stores, and before going to work each morning she would bring me in a lovely breakfast. I'd never known such luxury. Uncle did the shopping at the market; he was a dapper little fellow and was well known around the area. His shopping basket was a small suitcase, I never did find out why, but he was a good shopper. While I stayed with them I went shopping with him. What an education, what fun!

He took me to interesting places around Melbourne. I was impressed with the spaciousness and the clean wide streets. The sky seemed much higher too. The shops were overflowing with goodies, and he almost had to drag me past the butcher's shop – all that lovely meat! I hadn't ever seen so much. I remembered the tin of corned beef Mother was able to get from the butcher during the war, which was my week's supply.

We had family get togethers and I was made very welcome. I suppose they were curious about their English relative, but I loved the relaxed way of life of the Australian people.

Uncle had a friend who was a little older than he; he had always called Uncle 'Son', which I found very amusing. He was a retired detective sergeant in the police force, a colourful character, and one of his best stories was how he was involved in apprehending a well known criminal called Squizzy Taylor.

They would go about together and one day as they were going rabbiting, I was invited to tag along. 'Rabbits' brought too many memories for me, but I went with them.

Uncle did have a gun used solely for rabbiting, but he didn't always use it. He would walk slowly in the field and, passing a small tussock of grass, he would drop quickly to grab a rabbit which was squatting there, and dispatch it. There was no doubt that he was very agile and sharp for his age. I hadn't seen the rabbit there. I told him that he wasn't kind to the rabbit, he hadn't given it a sporting chance. But he said that shooting wasn't always successful, and if he missed actually killing it and it got away, it would have a slow painful death. I suppose there was some logic in his argument, but I didn't go with him again.

The English countryside was really beautiful, but in Australia I found a different beauty. The fields stretched for miles, but they weren't called fields but paddocks. The gum trees scattered around gave a scent of eucalyptus, and the tea-trees with their delicate flowers were everywhere. It was said that one could lift England completely and drop it in Victoria and there would still be space left over.

On one occasion, when visiting my male cousins who had a garage in Prahran, we decided to have fish and chips for lunch. I volunteered to get them. I was surprised to see the man put chips, which I thought were cooked, back into the hot fat. Thinking that he was using stale chips I refused to take them. Back at the garage this caused much laughter. In England the chips were cooked fresh. I went back to the shop and explained how chips were cooked in England. I'm sure he thought I was a nut; anyway his chips were delicious.

I had been in Australia for almost five weeks and it was time to think about getting a job. My hosts said that there was no hurry, but I felt it time to contribute money for my board, as I found it very difficult to give them anything – they just wouldn't accept it.

I went to the nurses' board in Melbourne to register and filled in a few forms, after which they said they would notify me when there was a vacancy. In the meantime I decided to apply to the Royal Melbourne Hospital, and how surprised I was to be asked to go for an interview. Everything happened so quickly – in no time at all, I found myself in uniform and on duty, and how good it felt!

For the first two weeks I was to overlap with the ward sister in a busy medical ward. Unfortunately she reported sick the following day. It took a little while to adjust to the different systems but the care of the patients was the same. During my stay there I was given every help possible.

At this time John had left Queensland to work in Yallourn, so that we were able to meet occasionally. As for Frostie, she was very homesick and longed to return. I realised how hard it must have been for her to leave her own home to share another. As for her husband Bert and daughter Doreen, both had good jobs; they were happy and loved Australia.

I received many invitations to visit and one weekend I accepted. They lived in West Geelong in a modest home, with Ted and his younger daughter. Plans had been made to go bush and have a barbecue. What a lovely day it was! Ted drove his station wagon which he had built himself. Apparently he had bought the engine for nine pounds and had built the body round it. I didn't take much notice of Ted except to think that he was rather clever. He was a wheelwright by trade and had completed his apprenticeship in England before migrating to Australia, at the age of twenty in 1924, where later he was employed by the Ford Motor Company.

I was given a huge piece of steak with onions, which had been cooked on an open fire covered with a metal rack. Could anything have tasted nicer? The smell wafted through the bush.

I lived in the nurses' home at the hospital but dropped in to visit Auntie and Uncle twice a week. We did a lot of talking and I was able to tell them what had happened after the 'big house', of the traumas and the miseries of our existence. Uncle had no answers except to say that we had just disappeared. I have asked myself why so many times, but we had survived; for me though there were a few scars that wouldn't heal.

John had settled in Yallourn about forty-five miles from Melbourne. He was a likeable fellow and we met when possible, and I took him to meet Uncle and Auntie. He said he was thinking of starting a poultry farm; I thought what a smelly job that would be. He never talked about his family and I wondered if he had a skeleton in the closet. Nevertheless we were good friends.

My trips to Geelong were always enjoyable and Frostie did her best to throw Ted and me together, so it was no surprise when he asked me my age. When I told him he made no comment, but he knew he was older than I. On one of my visits to join Auntie and Uncle I told them that the widower in Geelong was showing signs of being interest in me. She warned me to be careful, that he had two adult daughters and that it could be a very trying situation. She was Uncle's second wife and there were children involved and as she said it, I got the feeling that it hadn't been easy for her. I just laughed, saying there wasn't a problem. I wasn't ready to get involved with anyone, but I did continue to visit.

My first Christmas in Australia was so hot that I wilted. The wards at this time were decorated with bunches and bunches of flowers, and very early in the morning we went to the market. There was usually someone willing to drive, otherwise we went by taxi. I must admit the hospital corridors looked most attractive, and the wards were a colourful scene.

There was the usual carol service and Father Christmas came, bringing good cheer and a gift for each patient. It was most enjoyable and what a change from the English scene, with the cold and so often snow!

Quite a number of Melbourne houses heated their bath water with a contraption called a 'chip heater', a small cylinder with an opening near the bottom. It was perched on the side of the bath and one would have to feed it with wood chips. This heated the water, but I was pleased when a gas heater was installed for Auntie and Uncle. The chip heater was very economical, but it was a nuisance and very messy.

Uncle was a keen gardener and had a lovely veggie patch, and a green-house where he grew the best tomatoes I have ever eaten. Everything was kept in apple-pie order. There were a few widows in the neighbourhood, and it wasn't unusual for him for find a note in his letter box – 'Would you kindly cut my edge for me?'

I corresponded regularly with the folks at home. Mrs Wood and Marjorie were hoping that I would return at the end of the two years, which had been my plan. The curate had married the matron of a boy's home and was settled in his own parish.

It was on one of my visits to Geelong that we had a trip to Anglesea. Sitting on the beach, Ted asked if I could visit more often. He was extremely nice and I liked him a lot, we had much in common, but I wasn't sure that I wanted to go further. The attraction was there, but I really hadn't planned to stay in Australia. He didn't say very much, he certainly wasn't a talker. He confided that with Bert he had bought a block of land and that they planned to build a house in their spare time and maybe sell it. I smiled as I thought of his workshop, which was in a bad state of repair. There were thousands of cobwebs and I was convinced that the walls were held together by them.

I felt that I needed space, and when he asked if I could visit the following weekend I said that I was going to be busy, and I didn't visit for nearly three months. Surprisingly, I received a letter from Ted saying that he was planning a visit to the housing display at the Exhibition Building; as Bert and Frostie were coming too, he wondered if it would be possible for me to join them. As I was theatre sister at the hospital at that time and was off duty most weekends, I said that it wasn't a problem and that I would book seats at the Princess Theatre, the show being 'White Horse Inn'.

It was good to see them – I had missed them. The housing exhibition was interesting and I watched as Ted made notes. The show was excellent and during the interval Ted said, 'You are coming back with us,' to which I replied, 'Oh! no, thank you,' but Frostie was very persuasive, saying that I was expected, and that my bed was ready. I had no plans for the following day, which was Sunday, so accepted. There wasn't time to call at the nurses' home for nightclothes, but Frostie said not to worry as she could supply what I would need. It was the last train to Geelong that night and as time was on the wing, we had to hurry to catch it.

On arrival, Frostie and Bert disappeared to the kitchen to make a cup of tea leaving Ted and me alone. Our eyes met and after a few moments he said, 'Emily, you are going to marry me, aren't you?' I hadn't expected that and I certainly didn't expect to hear myself say, 'Yes.' It just seemed the right answer. Does fate play a part in our lives? I wonder! He didn't say he loved me, never did at all, there was no hugging and kissing, we just smiled as we looked at one another.

Frostie and Bert came in with the tea. I'm sure they felt the tension because when Ted told them, they congratulated us and said that it was what they had hoped for. There was very little sleep for me that night. I couldn't believe that I was to be married to that man, and I was anxious as to how his daughters would react to the news, but there wasn't a problem.

The following weekend Ted met Auntie and Uncle and they liked him immediately. Then we had to make plans for the future. There were many people to notify and the first was Matron at the Royal Melbourne Hospital. She was sorry I was leaving because she had hoped that I would relieve in the operating theatres. I didn't like the sound of that, as it was a big responsibility, and some of the surgeons were very hard to please. I realised what a demanding job they had but at least they could be polite. Nevertheless she accepted one month's notice.

I had really enjoyed my stay there, although coping with the shift work took some time to get used to. It was a good training school, well run, and I had extended my knowledge. I applied for a position as a midwife at a small maternity hospital in Geelong. I was accepted and could start immediately.

I wrote to John. He did know about Ted but apparently hadn't realised that the situation was serious; as a matter of fact neither did I, as it all happened so quickly. He wished us all the best. We heard from him on our wedding day but not again. I have often wondered about him; did he realise his dream of owning a small poultry farm? I sincerely hope so.

CHAPTER 25

The nursing home was very old, with eighteen beds; sometimes there were more. There were two labour wards. How happy I was to be back with mothers and babies! There was a snag, though; in Australia I was classed as a 'maternity nurse'. This meant that I was caretaker of the women until the time for the actual delivery. Each mother had her own doctor and some were terrible obstetricians. My responsibility was to ring for the doctor when the birth was imminent – not too soon and definitely not too late. The doctors in some cases were definitely too late and I quietly 'managed' very well.

It was a busy place which functioned well because of the dedicated staff as most were qualified maternity nurses. My salary at that time was nine pounds a week, and I felt very rich indeed. The plumber was always there as the pipes were often blocked. I wasn't a bit surprised as it was amazing what went down the drains.

Frostie and family moved out of the house in Geelong West, saying that now we would need to be alone. I wasn't happy about this but she insisted. We made plans for our wedding day and Ted worked hard to get the house shipshape; there was a lot to be done.

We were married on 2 September at three o'clock on a cold windy day and after the reception, Ted drove his station wagon along the Great Ocean Road to a small hotel where we were to stay for one week. My introduction to married life wasn't what I had imagined. How distorted are the stories that one hears! It certainly wasn't what I had dreamed about. Ted surprised me also; he was no Clark Gable as in 'Gone With The Wind'. Nevertheless we had plenty of time to work on this and we survived. We enjoyed walking and fishing – it was a lovely spot to stay, with beautiful scenery, but all too soon it was back to reality.

Ted's youngest daughter was to live with us for a while. She was good company and very busy completing a course at the local Technical

College. Ted was busy at his place of work, the Ford Motor Company, where he had been for a number of years. I saw very little of him, as he spent his evenings in his workshop. There appeared to be no togetherness, he didn't talk much and I was beginning to wonder why he had wanted to get married, then I found that I was pregnant. We were over the moon, as we had hoped to have two children.

I continued at the nursing home until I was five months pregnant and all seemed normal. Then suddenly the balloon burst. I had back pains and a high temperature. My own doctor was on holiday and the relief doctor, who was elderly, said that I had strained my back. He didn't examine me or test the specimen of urine I had taken. He got his prescription pad to order a pain killing tablet. I wasn't a bit impressed and said so, and walked out of the surgery.

Friends of the family were a young doctor and his wife. I had visited them frequently, helping with the birth of their second baby. Their first child had been stillborn. Ted said he would see him; I didn't think it was the right thing to do, but he went anyway. His diagnosis was pyelitis; I knew this and I was given a course of penicillin. Within a week I was better, but it wasn't to be, I had a relapse so was passed back to my own doctor who had returned from overseas.

Unfortunately I didn't respond to treatment and was forced to spend the rest of the time in bed. Ted was very patient – I wasn't. This was so very disappointing and there was nothing to do but to accept it.

During this time Rastus became my constant companion. I would make small balls with paper, throw them and he would bring them back to me. He was wonderful company. The 'Honourable Rastus', the cat, was in residence before I came on the scene. My step-daughters were very fond of animals and I gathered there had been a succession of cats, wandering in, aware that there would be food for them.

I hated bed rest, but I was up to the bathroom and toilet. My big worry was the little one I was carrying in my uterus, which was due to arrive on 17 August. Had it survived the high, swinging temperatures and the large doses of M&B693 I was given, which made me very sick? It was so disappointing for me. I had delivered so many healthy babies and hadn't had trouble with the mothers either. Why did this have to happen to me?

Frostie was very good and came daily and Ted's elder daughter, who was teaching at a high school, took compassionate leave for one month to look after me. How grateful I was, but what a nuisance I felt! I was on a special diet and one evening the smell of sausages cooking in the kitchen sent my taste buds into a frenzy, and I begged for just one inch. Meat was definitely not on my diet list, Frostie found this difficult to understand so it was not easy to adhere to.

On 17 August, my due date, there was no sign that my baby was ready to be born. It wasn't until just after midnight on the 23rd that I decided that I was definitely in labour. Realising that I was uncomfortable Ted flung back the bedclothes, and proceeded to get dressed.

'What are you doing'? I asked him.

'I'm going to take you to the nursing home.'

'You hop back into bed, there is nothing that they can do for me just yet.'

He grumbled, saying, 'You're going to leave it until the last minute?' He wasn't a happy man.

At five o'clock he drove me to the hospital. What a reception I got! 'Can't cope with you at the moment,' said my friend the night sister. 'It's been one of those nights.'

I said 'Goodbye' to Ted, who wasn't anxious to stay, then, rolling up my dressing gown sleeves, I cleaned both labour wards. I saw no one as I lay on the bed getting contractions every few minutes.

At 7.15 a.m., Ted popped in on his way to work and told the night sister that he would drive her home if she were finished.

'When do you think you will have the baby?' he asked.

'About 9 a.m.'

Night sister joined in; she scoffed. 'About 9 p.m. I should think.'

A little while later the membranes ruptured. In view of my history the doctor had wished to be informed when labour commenced. He was, just before the head was crowned. I know I did my share of grunting and shouting. Could anything be so painful? I was given a light anaesthetic before the actual birth, and I had to have stitches.

I thought of the mother with the toothless grin whom I had delivered on the district in London and how she had laughed as she had said that she was torn from 'Damn to Bethsheba' after each birth, and that the good 'ole doc', always fixed her up. Well I hoped the good 'ole doc' had fixed me up also. Through a mist when coming out of the anaesthetic I saw three sisters standing, each holding a baby. 'Congratulations,' they said, 'you've had triplets.' Perish the thought! I had a lovely baby boy born at 8.45 a.m. He weighed 7lbs 6oz and he was perfect. I shed a few tears and said a silent prayer; in my opinion pregnancy and giving birth had been no picnic.

When Ted saw his son he was delighted and I was highly amused as I watched him undress him. Satisfied that all was well he dressed him again. We named him Edward Herbert after Ted and his brother. I spent thirteen days in hospital and nursed a very sore bottom, but what a relief it was to have a normal diet again.

After seven weeks Edward was bottle fed on cow's milk. This was my fault, as I was weak and very tired. Thinking that my problems were over, I sort of dived in. However, when Edward was five months old I was admitted to hospital with a haemorrhage from the left kidney; except for rest there was no other treatment. I really was worried as I didn't feel well and seemed to be always visiting the doctor. Edward thrived; he wasn't a good feeder, but looked a bonny baby and we all loved him.

At this time I was very grateful to my younger step-daughter; not having had any experience with babies, it was amazing how she took over. She had said that Friday night was Ted's and my night together and that she would care for Edward. We took her up on her offer and occasionally went to the pictures.

The house Ted and his brother had been building was at the lockup stage and Ted suggested that we sell the house that we were living in and move there. Arrangements were made with Bert and Frostie and they received a cash settlement. Having bought two blocks of land, they planned with Ted's help to build their own home. This they did and were very happy with the result. It was no picnic living in the new house; there were no cupboards or doors, and only two bedrooms. Ted worked all day at the factory and at night in the home. I was very impatient and got tired of the noise and the mess, which didn't help my nerves.

I wasn't interested in sex; I feared a second pregnancy, realising that physically and mentally I was not ready. We talked about it and I shocked Ted by saying that if I did get pregnant I would have an abortion. He was absolutely horrified and said very firmly that there would be no abortion. I looked at that man and realised after eighteen months of marriage that there was a strong man with high moral ideals. I

113

assured him that I too had high ideals, but that I desperately wished to get back to my normal self. If only he had shown love and understanding, even just a cuddle, it would have helped but he wasn't like that. Was that feeling tucked away? Did he have it but not be able to show it? I never found out. We did coast along but it was not a very satisfactory sexual arrangement.

For a number of years I battled with kidney trouble and at one stage I was told I had a TB kidney. What shattering news that was! Doctor said the kidney would have to be removed and arrangements were made for me to enter hospital. The evening I was told I went down to the workshop to tell Ted – where else would I find him? He didn't seem unduly concerned and said, 'Why are you worried? You have two kidneys.' Of course I had learned very early in our marriage that I would never penetrate that steel composure and calm exterior. He loved his children and grandchildren, but I was confused and wondered exactly where I fitted into his life. I did point out that I hadn't been seen by a urologist, a kidney specialist. He said 'Why not?' Well, there wasn't one in Geelong and it would be expensive to travel to Melbourne. Nevertheless we decided to 'hang' the expense. I notified my doctor of our plans; he agreed that it was a good idea, and my bed was cancelled at the local hospital. We travelled to Melbourne by train and after numerous tests, the specialist said that although some part of the kidney was calcified it was functioning satisfactorily.

He was very puzzled as to where the diagnosis of TB kidney had come from, as he could not find tubercle bacillus in the urine. He said that a culture had proved this at the hospital but I was able to assure him that no culture had been done. On investigation it was found that an error had been made. I was to visit every three weeks for tests for almost two years. There was no change and providing that I took extra fluids and had a checkup every six months with my own doctor, I should continue as usual.

CHAPTER 26

As a young boy Edward got into mischief as little boys usually do. There were other children about his own age in the street so he wasn't lonely. The newly formed street had been part of an old property which had been sub-divided. As we were the first to build, it was interesting to watch other houses being built.

The block opposite had been sold and the owner, a keen gardener, had planted a number of gladioli bulbs. Imagine my horror when Edward, then three years old, presented me with what he called a bunch of 'onions'. He had pulled up her precious gladioli bulbs – they did resemble onions. I found that his two companions had helped, and their mother also received a bunch of 'onions'. Not knowing much about these bulbs, I replanted them, hoping that they would survive. When I saw the neighbour I explained what had happened. She was not impressed and reminded me that the children should not be allowed to wander as it was private property. Not a good introduction to a prospective neighbour! To save face and hopefully heal the rift, when gladioli were in season we ordered a large bunch to be delivered. Some of hers did survive, but it was a little while before we were accepted.

When Edward started school, I decided that I needed an interest. There was a vacancy at a local girl's college for a nursing sister. I applied and was lucky to be accepted but it was only as a relief because they needed a sister full time. I couldn't do this because of my family commitments.

There were many boarders, and what a difference it was from my usual nursing duties! The general routine was replaced by a needs programme, and I dealt with the problems as they arose. Every morning I would open the dispensary and was surprised at the many problems with which some of the girls had to cope. I needed to be a good listener, sympathetic and very approachable.

One young student came to see me every morning for a few days. I could see no sign of a physical problem, but I sensed that she was deeply troubled about something. I had a chat to her mother on the phone, but she was reluctant to say what she thought the problem was. Apparently the girl had been made to stand out in class and, being very emotional, thought she was being laughed at. I assured her mother that I would be very tactful, and the form teacher was surprised when I told her. She did say that maybe she had been a little harsh, hadn't really attached much importance to the incident. It was a different girl who came to see me two days later.

One of my duties was to sit at the head of one of the dining room tables to carve the meat and, much to the girls' amusement, I wasn't very good at it; when it came to my turn, I had run out of meat. Any finicky eaters had to sit at the principal's table. Conversation was encouraged.

Unfortunately for me, after a few months a full time nursing sister was appointed. I was reluctant to leave. I felt very sorry for some of the young boarders, especially those who were there full time. Activities were organised for them, they were well supervised, but they missed the love of their family.

My next nursing position was part-time in a geriatric nursing home. How impressed I was with the care given! There were different cases and a few acute medical cases, and all were given tender loving care. I had to resign just before Christmas because we always camped at a nearby beach for two and a half weeks. I didn't think that this was much of a holiday – cooking meals on a kerosene stove, carrying the water from the tap nearby and crawling in the hedge to retrieve cutlery that I had thrown out with the washing up water. Ted said I didn't have the pioneering spirit. But there was a plus; with no house work, I could relax and catch up with some reading. For thirteen years we returned to that same spot each Christmas.

With the help of a friend we organised a beauty contest, which was most successful, and on New Year's Day there were family sports and a fishing contest. Everyone joined in. Occasionally we were treated to a film on the beach, each person taking a stool or chair and a rug. I collected round the camp for money which was used for prizes.

CHAPTER 27

In October 1969, after forty-three years, Ted retired from the Ford Motor Company, where for the last few years he had been the employment officer. I wondered what next, knowing full well that he was a workaholic. He had been home for only a few days when he was asked if he would take over a local sheltered workshop.

All I could think of was, 'Here we go again.' Not asking me what I thought, he immediately said 'Yes,' and he took over the following week. He was sixty-five years old.

For the next ten years it was heavy going as he worked so hard and so did I, using the dining room as an office. He was able to secure contracts from some of the local firms and the kindergartens in and around Geelong. They were big customers. Nothing was beyond him, no request too small, and starting with only four men he was eventually able to increase to fifty. The men, some disabled through accidents, others with problems, were very happy.

They were good workers and the small salary they got didn't bother them; they were working and eager to please. After some time a few were able to return to the work force. I remember one of the parents saying to me one day, 'Take your Teddy home, he'll kill himself.' What could I say except that he was doing what he wanted to, always had, and there wasn't anything I could do about it? He retired at the age of seventy-eight.

It was during this time that I heard that my mother had died, at the age of seventy-six. Her last years had been very comfortable, as she had a lovely self-contained unit. Dorothy had cared for her; she had always been by Mother's side.

Edward studied the science course at the local technical school and did well. He applied to do an apprenticeship in instrumentation at a local factory. In this he was very successful and he qualified as an instrument technician. He was invited by the firm to further his career and do an engineering course, but he decided to go out in the workforce. After travelling overseas to gain experience, he eventually settled down to marry a delightful girl, and has become the proud father of twins.

Ted's daughters made their own way in life; each married and they had nine children between them. They had had their usual family problems.

My last nursing position was with the association for the blind. This was a marvellous organisation, as blind and partially blind people were able to enjoy a day out at the centre. They took part in many activities and were taught by the staff, who were so helpful. I looked after any medical problems, kept medical records, and visited them in their own homes.

It was some time later that I was told that a doctor was joining the staff. He was returning to the work force after suffering a major stroke. When I first saw him I thought how ill he looked, but his bright personality shone through, and later I found that he had a wonderful sense of humour. Dr Ames was an instant success. It didn't take the blind members long to realise that here was a doctor who was caring and understanding, and who was also a very good listener. He was kept very busy.

What a thrill it was to hear that he had completed his training at the London Hospital, and he asked if I knew his sister who was also a trainee. Of course I did. I wanted to put my arms around his neck and give him a big hug. With his wife, also a London Hospital trainee, and four boys he had left England to settle in Apollo Bay, a nearby seaside resort. There he had been the general dogsbody. He was popular as a doctor, surgeon, midwife and even vet; it seems that nothing was too much trouble for him.

I was very pleased to meet his wife Joan, a very courageous little woman who had coped with the trauma of his medical problems. It was so noticeable that she was always by his side and looking over his shoulder. It was a very busy time for her, with four schoolboys to care for as well.

I was still having medical problems, and the tablets I was given to take were not helping, even when they were increased. I just couldn't cope and eventually dropped my bundle. I had become addicted to the tablets and was a nervous wreck. I realised that this was serious, and that I desperately needed help.

We had booked to travel to England but I wasn't in a fit state to travel. Ted, his usual calm self, patted me on the back, saying, 'You'll be all right', but all right I wasn't.

It was then that I asked Dr Ames for help. As he listened, he said how mystified he was that I had allowed myself to get into such a state. I put myself entirely in his hands, and what a relief that was! He discontinued the tablets I had been taking and ordered a low dose tranquilliser. It wasn't easy, but he was firm, kind and very encouraging. His wife was a frequent visitor to our house also and, in spite of her busy programme, gave me all the help possible, so that on the scheduled date we boarded the plane for England.

Dr Ames had arranged for his brother-in-law, a well known psychiatrist in the Midlands, and his wife to meet the plane at Heathrow. I had known him during the war at Billericay where he had been an intern at the hospital. His wife, Dr Ames' sister, gave me a big hug and except for being older they hadn't changed.

It was a lovely feeling to be taken home by these two dear people. I believe I slept twelve hours. The flight had been long and tedious and it seemed that we were always eating.

We stayed with them for four days and during that time we had long talks. His conclusion was that even though I was partly to blame for my nervous condition, the treatment I had been given had been most unsatisfactory. Nevertheless he said to continue the treatment given by Dr Ames, and should I need him as we went on our travels, he was at the end of the phone. I didn't, but I did keep in contact.

For seven weeks we travelled, visiting friends and relatives. Ted was excited as it had been about sixty years since he left to sail on the *Largs Bay* for Australia.

He was surprised how little things had changed, and when he visited the infant school he had attended as a boy and sat in his former seat, it did cause a great deal of amusement. The building had become the home of the Women's Voluntary Association.

It was a most successful trip and although we loved England and our friends there we were happy to return to Australia.

Marjorie's mother had died at the age of ninety-two. Marjorie had married and with her husband had spent two holidays with us, which was a great joy.

The phone rings and I get up to answer it; it is Edward to say that he will visit tomorrow. This pleases us greatly; the twins, now six years old, are a delight and so full of mischief. Margaret their mother is very capable; I never see the kitchen sink while she is here.

Well, I must get lunch, the tummies must be fed and my dreaming time is over.

We have weathered the storms, each achieving a great deal. Naturally it hasn't been easy.

Time is on the wing, we are well aware that every day is a bonus and we will appreciate this and exploit it to the full.

We can both say . . .

'IT WASN'T SO BAD AFTER ALL.'